HIDDEN
BUDDHISM

HOW TO LIVE WITH MAXIMUM IMPACT
AND MINIMUM EGO

LACHLAN BROWN

Contents

Part Three: Using Buddhism for a Better Life

INTRODUCTION

I've got a hard question for you: Are you happy and fulfilled in life?

If you'd asked me five years ago, my honest answer would have been no.

My answer today is absolutely, unequivocally YES. As I write this, I'm living with purpose, embracing my flaws and being authentic about where I fall short. I'm succeeding in a way I never thought possible.

I still have down days, of course. Frustrated times. I'm sure you do too. But I finally feel like I'm living. And I mean, really living. I even love the tough times, because now I know how to get through them and do something useful with them instead of just languishing in misery.

Here's the truth: The old me wouldn't even recognize me today.

How did I go from struggling to thriving? What made the difference and why? And what does it take to get to this point?

There's no complicated formula here, but there is a set of steps I took to make this happen, and a lot of the credit goes to the teachings of Buddhism.

I've found out how to apply the ancient secrets of Buddhism to modern life in a way that truly works. These secrets helped me unlock the life of my dreams, and become content and excited about living in the present.

In this book, I'm going to tell you all about that and how this can be your narrative, too. I'm going to reveal what I learned by studying and applying lesser-known teachings and real truths of Buddhism, and combining it with my background in psychology.

You might be wondering, "What can Buddhism really offer me?" It's a valid question, especially if your daily grind feels worlds away from serene meditations and ancient texts.

But here's the thing: the core teachings of Buddhism can be incredibly relevant to our modern lives. They teach us how to handle stress, how to detach from unhealthy desires, and how to appreciate the present moment – skills that are invaluable whether you're a CEO or a stay-at-home parent. Or someone who feels like life is meaningless, like I used to be.

For me, the principles of mindfulness and acceptance were game-changers. I'll be honest: Life used to kick my ass. Every day it gave me a royal beating and left me feeling victimized and alone. Life happened to me. Now I happen to life, thanks to these principles. They taught me to find a sense of contentment not from external achievements, but from within. I was shocked to realize that I could find peace and beauty even while working at a job that felt soul-crushing in the beginning!

Imagine not being swayed by every setback or chasing every fleeting pleasure, but instead, finding a steady peace regardless of circumstances. That's what learning about and practicing Buddhist principles can do for you.

This is what I want to stress: None of where I am today happened by accident. You see, everything is created through intent.

Let me also clear something up: I'm not a religious person. I'm not a Buddhist, and you don't need to be either to follow these teachings. But I like to do what works, and what I talk about in this book worked for me. That's why I'm going to share it with you.

I'm going to reveal how putting into action the teachings of Eastern philosophy and Buddhism helped take me from being a frustrated single man unloading shipping containers for minimum wage in Australia…

… To running one of the world's leading websites in mindfulness and Eastern philosophy, with 15 million monthly readers and 200,000 e-mail subscribers…

… And living in Vietnam, happily married to my beautiful wife Jess, experiencing the kind of financial freedom the old me could only dream of.

Maybe you're in a place right now where things feel like they're not working out for you, and you fear this will be your reality forever.

I get it: When you're in the midst of struggle, it's natural to lose sight of the bigger picture and not be able to see your challenges as just a snapshot in time. It can feel like there's no way out.

But there is. If you're scared that things can't get better, know that they can and will – as long as you're willing to learn and make the changes needed. It's about taking your present, practical situation and maximizing it into an experience that's actually worth living.

This book is a great starting point for that. It's the result of years of putting ancient wisdom to the test in our busy, modern world. It will give you practical skills and real answers, not long-winded philosophical musings. What you'll find here instead – accessible and actionable advice grounded in sound Buddhist teachings.

At its heart, Buddhism is about understanding the causes of suffering and how to alleviate them through self-awareness and ethical living. It's about individual practice and enlightenment — figuring out your own path to being happier and more aware of the world around you.

This is pretty refreshing, especially if you're tired of the usual religious routines. Buddhism is more about self-improvement and living a richer, more satisfying life day by day, no matter who you are or what your situation is.

By understanding the Four Noble Truths and how the Eightfold Path of Buddhism plays out in everyday life, anyone – from an atheist to a devout Christian to a Buddhist – can make these principles work for them.

In this book, we'll dive into how you can use these ideas to really take charge of your life, feel more connected, and find a deep, lasting peace.

Now, I can't promise to fix all your problems – I don't claim to be enlightened, nor holier-than-thou. But I can promise to help those problems make a lot more sense and help you see opportunities where you formerly saw only closed doors.

I hope you'll join me on this journey.

Lachlan Brown
July 22, 2024
Saigon, Vietnam

*

PART ONE
The Four Noble Truths

*

CHAPTER ONE

*The Inescapable Reality
(Dukkha | Life is Suffering)*

"The noble truth of suffering (dukkha) is this: birth is suffering; aging is suffering; sickness is suffering; death is suffering; sorrow and lamentation, pain, grief, and despair are suffering; association with the unpleasant is suffering; disassociation from the pleasant is suffering; not to get what one wants is suffering. In brief, the five aggregates of attachment are suffering."

Siddharta Gautama Buddha

T here I was, a 26-year-old university graduate lifting boxes in a warehouse. My lower back was aching as I helped unload the last of a large order of flat screen TVs from a 40-foot shipping container.

It was going to be another long, long day. I took a quick drink of water and scanned my lengthy checklist, stifling the inner groan that rose up like a reflex from inside. There was a lot more that needed doing by the end of today. My stomach growled. It was almost break, and I had a ham sandwich that was calling my name. At least there was that to look forward to …

This had started as a stopgap job at 24, something to pay the bills while I found my direction in life. At first, the job had been fine, although the "logistics" title that had drawn my initial attention had been a little off the mark.

I'd put my back into the work and I'd done my best. I'd seen the positive side of getting a working man's Ph.D. But the novelty had worn off. This was backbreaking work, and any sheen of adventure had worn off.

Two years into it, and no other opportunities had presented themselves. I'd applied to plenty of positions, of course. But new jobs weren't exactly jumping off the shelves and running towards me with their arms outstretched. My degree in psychology also hadn't turned out to be the selling feature I'd hoped it would be when I graduated. So, for now, it was me and the shipping containers.

I'd spent those two years dreaming of something better, dreading waking up in the morning and basically wishing I was "anywhere but here." The desire to be anywhere other than where I was had me on edge, irritable, and feeling very off-kilter.

I wanted more out of life. I wanted to feel like my daily routine was meaningful beyond grinding it out in the 9-to-5 rat race in a forgettable industrial area of Melbourne.

After the first six months, I started having a lot of trouble sleeping and experienced depressive thoughts about the future on an ongoing basis. I felt like life was passing me by, especially when I heard of friends scoring amazing careers, getting married and living the kinds of lives I'd always dreamed about.

At night, I'd lie awake in bed, thinking, *When would it be my turn?*

I'd always been a happy-go-lucky guy, but my level of chill was at an all-time low. I felt frayed. Increasingly serious anxiety was tripping me up as I thought of the future. It was like staring into a black hole with no end. Two years in and I was about to ready tap out.

But where to go and what to do, exactly?

Now, my life wasn't completely terrible — I had my family, cool coworkers, and a comfy bed to sleep in at night. I don't want to sound like an ungrateful git because I know the world is full of people who have it worse-off than I did. But my life just wasn't going anywhere. I felt like a plane stuck in an endless holding pattern.

Was this depression or did my life just suck?

I was a young person full of questions and in search of answers. I was brimming with complaints and pain, and looking for satisfaction.

As alone as I felt back then, I know now that my situation wasn't unique. I think this is where a lot of us live – in anxiety, pain, a seemingly permanent state of uncertainty. Just like me, many of us are caught in jobs that drain us, relationships that don't fulfill us, or circumstances that seem to trap us.

Understanding Dukkha

In a little village in ancient India, there was a young woman named Kisa Gotami. She was super sweet and everyone in the village loved her. She was over the moon when she had a baby boy, — her life seemed perfect. But then, something awful happened — her baby got really sick and, despite everything she tried, he passed away.

Kisa Gotami was absolutely heartbroken. She couldn't accept that her baby was gone, so she carried him around the village, asking anyone and everyone if they had some medicine to bring him back to life. The villagers felt terrible for her and suggested she go see the Buddha, who was known for his incredible wisdom.

Desperate for help, Kisa Gotami found the Buddha and begged him for a remedy to bring her son back. The Buddha listened kindly and said, "I can help you, but first you need to bring me a mustard seed from a house that hasn't faced death."

Thinking this would be easy, Kisa Gotami went from door to door, asking for a mustard seed. But at every house, she heard the same thing — each family had experienced loss and death in some way. No house was untouched by sorrow.

As she visited more homes, Kisa Gotami started to realize something important. Everyone, no matter who they were, had experienced suffering. It wasn't just her. By the end of the day, she understood what the Buddha had been trying to tell her.

She went back to the Buddha, still holding her son, but now with a new understanding. The Buddha gently explained, "You see, you're not alone in your grief. Suffering is a part of life for everyone. Recognizing this helps us find compassion and wisdom."

Kisa Gotami, enlightened by this truth, buried her son and decided to follow the Buddha. She spent the rest of her life helping others understand the nature of suffering and how to find peace despite it.

This is the **First Noble Truth of Buddhism - life is suffering.**

It may sound bleak, but it's crucial for understanding our existence. It's not negativity; it's reality. As the story above shows, all of us go through suffering. Pain, loss, disappointment, and unfulfilled desires are universal. These experiences shape and challenge us and help us grow.

And the sooner we accept this truth, the better.

You see, acknowledging suffering is the first step to overcoming it. Buddhism teaches us that the way out of suffering is to understand it as an inherent aspect of life.

In other words, until we learn to accept its natural existence in human life, we'll always be suffering in one form or another. We'd be stuck in cycles of blame, denial, anger, and self-pity!

By accepting that life is suffering, we release unrealistic expectations and find peace in reality. We can begin to appreciate small moments and lessons from hardship.

We can then manage to see its roots — our desires, clinging to temporary pleasures, and avoiding pain.

Where do you feel the most discontented? Your job, relationships, or self-expectations?

The Buddha emphasized that the suffering of life does not mean you should bliss out or become indifferent about life. This is actually a common misunderstanding of his teaching.

So let's clarify that:

Acceptance of suffering empowers you to take control of your inner world. To not let external things steer you in directions you don't want to go. Instead, it's about mindfully doing and taking actions without basing your worth or happiness on the outcome.

If someone tries to make you angry, let them. Accept it without getting angry. If life seems to be conspiring against you to beat you down, let it. You don't need to lose spirit or become bogged down.

Despite how it sounds, the first Noble Truth isn't about passivity or despair. It's an invitation to awaken, see life as it is, and embrace both joy and pain. The point is to live authentically, engage deeply with life, and become more compassionate and resilient to setbacks.

My journey out of that warehouse wasn't quick. It didn't happen with a snap of the fingers. It happened slowly, day by day. It happened when I began to focus on actions, and finding a still place inside where I could stop dreaming so much of the future and start maximizing my present.

Any outer success I have originated in one specific place:

Learning to get to know suffering and make it my friend and teacher instead of my enemy.

Instead of seeing everything as a roadblock, I began to see things as opportunities for character growth. The way I worked changed. My inner life became more tranquil and rich and I started to unload boxes with pride and intention, making friends with what *was* instead of what I wished would be. I even came to find the rhythm of loading and unloading boxes soothing, even though it's hard physical labor.

This is what you have to be prepared to do, if you're serious about turning your life around – make peace with suffering and see it as just a natural part of life.

One key thing many people may not know:

The Buddhist symbol for enlightenment is the **lotus flower**, and the mud and grime that feeds into its brilliant flower is the mess of our lives. We all have mess and mud down there!

But that mud is what lets our roots grow. It's where we draw our nourishment from. You have to love (or at least appreciate) the mud, not just tolerate it.

Be honest and confront your "mud". Your thoughts and feelings have value — even when they are unpleasant to face. As Buddhist monk Thich Nhat Hanh says, you have to "touch the pain."

As you touch your pain, it will hurt at first, but you'll feel lighter. It's as if when you touch it, you massage it and release the tension. The path upward starts with reaching your roots into that murky cesspool of subconscious chaos.

You'll find unexpected nutrients, like inner strength, determination, realism, patience, maturity, a sense of humor, appreciation for small things…

Sounds good, right? Believe me, it is, though it might not feel that way at first.

Here's a truth truly worth noting — none of us are getting out of here alive. We have to face our mortality and the reality of suffering to shape our lives into something meaningful and worthwhile.

If you hide from life, life will hide from you and only pain will find you. Learn to float somewhere in the space between the sky and the mud without craving pleasure and running from discomfort.

Nothing I wished for came true until I stopped depending on it for my inner happiness. So live with non-attachment. Identify what truly matters to you. Write it down in a journal.

Enjoy being in your flow without pressure.

It's the foundation for what comes next.

With that in mind, let's do an exercise …

EXERCISE ONE
Life's a Bitch..Or is It?

Get a white poster board and divide it in two columns as follows. Get a marker and write down answers to the following questions.

Pain	Pleasure
• What is causing you the most pain right now in life?	• What is making you the happiest right now?
• What do you hate most about it?	• What do you love most about it?
• How does it make you feel?	• How does it make you feel?
• How does it worry you?	• How does it make you hopeful?
• How does it victimize you?	• How does it empower you?
• How does it limit you and hold you back?	• How does it expand your horizons?

Advantages of this Pain	Disadvantages of this Pleasure
• What are the top strengths and skills you can gain from this pain you are going through?	• How can what is making you happiest right now actually make you weaker in some ways?
• How can your hate of what you're suffering from help build you as a person?	• What are some ways in which your love of this experience, person, or thing could be leaving you open to disappointment or dependency?
• How can your angry, sad or confused feelings about this experience feed into your future mission?	
• How can worrying about this help you become a better planner for the next decision you make?	• How upset would you be if you lost what you love? Would you feel your life is over?
• How can this experience of being victimized make you stronger?	• Are you basing your happiness on this thing that brings you pleasure? That leaves you very vulnerable!
• How can the limitations of this suffering you are going through bring you more humility and patience?	• Are you counting on life continuing to go your way in this regard? Couldn't this open you up to being badly blindsided?

What's the point?

Everything you think is awful and intolerable has the chance to build you into a more realistic and determined person.

Everything bringing you pleasure and making you take life for granted has the potential to build you into a weaker and less realistic person.

Of course, sometimes pain is just pain, and pleasure is just pleasure. But what we do with it often leads us astray, and that's the point here.

If you're deep in the mud right now, remember: it's not forever. By working through this book, you're on the production line to becoming a much stronger, more effective person.

*

CHAPTER TWO

Breaking Free (Samudaya | The Origin of Suffering)

"People suffer because they are caught in their views. As soon as we release those views, we are free and we don't suffer anymore."

Thich Nhat Hanh

S o, we've already established that suffering is a natural occurrence in life. But why exactly is that? Why do we suffer?

The answer is in the **Second Noble Truth**: suffering is caused by **attachment**.

This is sometimes translated as being caused by desire.

We all have plenty of desires. I did then and I still do now, and I imagine it's the same for you. And if we're not careful, those desires can easily lead us astray.

For example, our craving for more money can push us to exploit others. Our longing for love or pleasure can trap us in toxic relationships. Our hunger for power can turn us into someone we're not proud of. We're always reaching, always wanting more, and that constant chase can make us miserable because we miss out on enjoying what's already in front of us.

Thinking of myself back in that warehouse, I had so many desires – a better job, a better love life, more money, and more respect from others. I wanted to be thinner, have a nicer apartment and have money to travel. I wanted a lot, and not getting it was driving me mad.

But I wanted it in the wrong way: I wanted it to come toward me from outside, not to generate it from my own focus and actions.

If I could just get that one big break, I would finally be able to prove my worth to the world, get the girl who was meant for me, become the psychological researcher who helped solve the world's problems.

That "one big break" – I *deserved* that, and more.

I would lay awake at night fantasizing about a life where I'd truly get what I "deserved." What's more, the greater the focus on what I was owed and what the world should be giving me, the worse I felt.

Does this sound familiar?

Here's the obvious and uncomfortable truth:

No external accomplishment can make you love yourself. No outer love can fill a hole you feel inside. No outer validation can fill an insecurity you're too scared to fill yourself. The more you live in a world of expectations and attachments, the more you will suffer unnecessarily. The more you depend on the outside to make you happy inside, the more miserable and desperate you will become.

Besides, the world doesn't owe us anything, and to think so would be a sure path to suffering.

So, what does this really mean and how can we apply it to our lives? There's no button we can press to stop wanting what we want, right?

The Nature of Attachment

New Age Law of Attraction talks all about attracting what you mirror and so on, but, in my opinion, it's just not true. Life has many factors, including karma, that draw all sorts of different experiences our way. Life also has physical laws, which means we don't always get all we need and definitely not all we want.

Buddhism is straight up honest about this. Disappointment and pain are part of everyone's life. But being disappointed and in pain about being disappointed and in pain is a different thing completely. In other words, the emotions of pain, fear, and resentment come to us all. But weaving a story around them and believing they are personal or deeply directed at you is optional. This realism is what attracted me most to Buddhism in the first place: it's about practical wisdom, not analysis and philosophical hair-splitting.

Unhealthy attachment is all about clinging to a satisfying illusion and thinking life owes you one. It's exactly what I did during those two miserable years of my life.

In contrast, healthy detachment is all about doing your best in life but still fully accepting that life doesn't owe you anything, and even if it did, there's no guarantee you would get it.

Attachment is throwing away your gear and quitting football when you lose a big game, and suffering for months in disappointment and anger.

Meanwhile, an end to attachment is continuing to play the next season with even more energy and enthusiasm for the love of the game.

See the difference?

This is where Buddhism digs deeper. It's not just the desires themselves; it's our attachment to them that trips us up. We cling to our wants, our loves, and our beliefs in a world where nothing is permanent. We often suffer because we hold on too tightly to people, things, and ideas.

Our evolutionary brains are designed for survival and accumulating rewards. But if we don't develop stronger discipline and vision than our primal self, we become lost in a life of random rewards and punishments.

Think about it like a sandcastle – if you hold it too tightly, it crumbles. But if you enjoy it without clinging, you can appreciate its beauty without suffering when it eventually washes away. This idea is at the very heart of Buddhist teaching, and it may take a little time to get your head around. But it's a great way to understand the Buddhist view of suffering.

Once you really grasp this concept, it starts to shift how you view everything. Life becomes less about holding on and forcing things and more about experiencing it all with a light touch. And this, for me, was the seismic change that really led me to a different way of being and living.

I learned to take charge of my desires and attachments instead of letting them drive me. I learned to stop relying on life to bring me what I want or provide me with satisfaction and freedom.

This is key if you want to genuinely turn your life around.

If we let our desires rule our lives and our attachments form our priorities, it's like running a marathon with heavy weights around your ankles. Once you take charge of your desires and attachments instead of letting them run you, you fling those weights off and become the Usain Bolt of personal development.

But before you can do that, are you even aware of what your desires are and what's actually driving your agenda?

Are you able to identify whether the prospect of not achieving desires of yours triggers a feeling of having wasted your life?

Are you, for example, absolutely bound to these "ingredients for a happy life"?

- Getting married
- Achieving acclaim for your work
- Buying a house
- Standing on a stage and giving a talk

Don't feel stupid for having these thoughts – coming to terms with them allows you to start letting go and move on from them.

Getting these thoughts down on paper will help you get clarity. Have a long think about why these things seem so important to you. As you reflect on your desires and attachments, bring awareness to the need to not rely on them to bring you happiness. That's not to say you stop caring about what happens: a better future, a chance at love, a place you can call home…

You simply stop thinking it will bring you inner satisfaction and peace. It won't!

Now, I know it sounds like it's something so easy to do. "Simply stop" can be a misleading statement. After all, if it was that easy, then none of us would be walking around with heavy balls of despair and longing in our chests, right? Learning to just exist sounds ridiculous, but it's one of the toughest things any of us can learn to do.

For me, it started with a mindset reset. I had to accept that clinging, desire-filled part of me, the emotions of anger and sadness about not getting what I "deserved". But I also had to stop believing that these desires were my core identity or that they would bring me what I really sought.

If you're in a similar position, I encourage you to do the same.

The key here is to understand the difference between acceptance and belief. You must accept that these emotions and responses are a valid part of your growing and learning experience. And of course, you should go on working hard and striving to be the best you can be. However, you must resist the belief that some future point or ideal will solve all your problems or bring you to achieve your dreams. You can't hinge your happiness on external factors and do things in life as part of a kind of deal.

It was only once I began to truly give up on a better future arriving and a golden ideal that this better future truly began to approach and start happening. It was only by opening up space in the present and a stabilized, neutral self that I began to see new opportunities and room to grow. Talk about irony!

Instead of being so stuck in my head, a victim of whatever thoughts and desires popped up, I focused on developing the emotional and mental discipline to exercise more self-control through mindfulness and meditation practices. I'll talk more about this in a later chapter.

Instead of expectations, I started applying daily effort. Instead of future prizes I wanted to win, I started focusing on present realities.

The result was that I started to feel much more energized in myself. The warehouse job still wasn't my dream job, but I started to really feel grateful for the hardworking people who surrounded me, for my parents who loved me, for my body, which kept me walking and healthy. I began seeing life as a net plus instead of a net loss.

I still had my low moments, of course. But I no longer felt this inadequacy and dependency for it to happen in order for me to be enough. I felt more secure in myself; that awareness slowly spread through me at a physical and emotional level, aided enormously by my meditative practice as well. I stopped looking for anyone to help me or come save me. I became focused on *contributing* instead of what I could get.

Even today, my monkey mind still chatters away and swings around on my neural pathways now and then, but I no longer give it as much credit and seriousness as I used to. It's not that my desires died away either. It's that I stopped believing they would bring me happiness and satisfaction.

You might not believe this can happen to you…but with a mindfulness practice, you'll observe a shift in your thinking. You'll learn to begin living in the present moment instead of constantly needing to label it, analyze it, and "get" something from it.

As you get better at it, you'll see that this old adage is true: "Pain is certain; suffering is optional."

EXERCISE TWO
Shout at the Devil

- Get a stack of biodegradable paper.
- On each sheet, write down one thing that you consider very good, bad, or potentially good or bad in your life.
- For example: "one day I will die." "I love my girlfriend so much." "I'm so hopeful about getting a better job at the firm next month." "I'm worried I might have a serious illness." "I'm fucked up and see no point in my life continuing."
- Write it all down – one issue or noteworthy thing that's on your mind on each page.
- Next, make or purchase a piñata. Instructions for making one are easily found online and materials are cheap to buy.
- Make a hole in it with a knife and put every piece of paper inside with your hopes and fears on them. All your suffering and joy.
- Buy a baseball bat. Aluminum or wood, it doesn't matter.
- Put on a pair of good shoes and walk to a place where nobody else is around, such as a forest or remote campsite.
- Bring an external speaker and your phone.

- Create a playlist full of music that speaks to you and gets you emotional: happy, sad, furious, laughing out loud.
- Hit play, and play it loud.
- Shout, cry, laugh, cackle like a goddamn madman or madwoman. Howl like a wolf. Dance around in a tribal frenzy. Rock out like a metalhead at a deafening concert.
- Hit the shit out of that piñata and watch all your desires, hopes, fears, and attachments scatter all over as flakes of that lovely biodegradable paper.

What's the point?

You've just shouted at the devil. Consider it a metaphor. Everything you are attached to will be gone one day, even *you*.

You've gotta let that shit go!

In one way or another, non-attachment is about getting a bit more into your body and the moment, and letting all the expectations and hopes and fears float on the wind.

I know of no better way that having a one-person piñata party with a great soundtrack.

*

CHAPTER THREE

Choosing Action Over Agony
(Nirodha | The Ending of Unnecessary Suffering)

"The experience of nirvana marks a turning point in an individual's life, not a final and immutable goal. After the experience one knows that one is free not to act on the impulses that naturally arise in reaction to a given situation. Whether one chooses to act on impulses is another matter."

Stephen Batchelor,
"After Buddhism: Rethinking the Dharma for a Secular Age"

fter that big question of where suffering comes from comes another big question: How do we change this mess we're in?

We usually have two moves – avoid the problem or face it head-on. Like, if someone's making your life miserable, you stay away from them, right? Or if you hate where you live, you might think about moving. But it's never that easy.

Take me, for instance, stuck in that dead-end warehouse job. I was desperate to get out, but didn't know how or even what "getting out" really meant. So, I tried escaping in small ways, like counting down the minutes until I could zone out watching Australian Rules Football and forget the day's stress. Sometimes, I'd go drinking with my buddies after work, then wake up with a terrible hangover. My job felt like a prison, and like a lot of folks, I felt trapped by my need for cash – to eat, to pay rent, and all that.

Buddhism does not dismiss all these experiences we go through. The Buddha understood that not everyone can just escape the tough parts of life. Big stuff like pain, sickness, death – no one can dodge those.

But he did have an answer: *Nirodha*, the **third Noble Truth** of Buddhism. It's all about realizing that you can end your own suffering.

And how exactly do you do that? Let go. Let go your cravings, your wishes for something better – be it a job, an exciting life, or nicer stuff. Let go of wanting to escape.

Sounds tough, right? It was for me too, at first. But when I really took this to heart, it changed how I saw my awful situation. I started to really pay attention to what I was doing, even the mundane task of unloading boxes. And as I've told you earlier, there's a kind of beauty, a grace even, in the simplest tasks when you're fully in the moment. The Buddha's teachings helped me deal with the daily grind without feeling crushed by it. All the tough stuff – the back pain, the restless nights – it was all nothing more than the mud my lotus was reaching down into to grow its roots. It was just the dirt where my future happiness was starting to grow.

That realization was my turning point, and it has an official name – *nirvana*.

The State of Nirvana

In the time of Siddartha Guatama, there was a notorious bandit named Angulimala. He was feared by everyone because of his ruthless ways. Angulimala had a twisted goal: to collect a thousand fingers from his victims, thinking it would bring him great power.

One day, as Angulimala was hiding in the forest, he heard that the Buddha was nearby. Curiosity got the better of him, and he decided to find this Buddha everyone talked about. As the Buddha walked calmly along a path, Angulimala appeared and demanded that the Buddha stop.

But the Buddha kept walking, serene and unafraid. Angulimala shouted, "Stop, monk!" The Buddha calmly replied, "I have stopped, Angulimala. It is you who have not stopped."

Confused and intrigued, Angulimala asked what he meant. The Buddha explained, "I have stopped causing harm to others and to myself. I have found peace and ended my suffering. You, Angulimala, are still trapped in a cycle of violence and suffering."

Angulimala was struck by the Buddha's words. No one had ever spoken to him like this before. He felt a deep shift inside him and realized that his path of violence was causing him immense suffering. He asked the Buddha how he could find peace.

The Buddha taught Angulimala about the third noble truth: the end of suffering. He explained that by letting go of hatred, greed, and ignorance, and by following a path of compassion and mindfulness, one could achieve a state of peace and freedom from suffering.

Angulimala, deeply moved, decided to change his ways. He threw away his weapons and chose to follow the Buddha. He joined the Buddha's community of monks and dedicated his life to making amends and helping others.

Over time, Angulimala became known for his kindness and wisdom. He experienced firsthand that the end of suffering was possible, and he shared this truth with everyone he met.

A **state of peace and freedom from suffering** – that's exactly what ***nirvana*** is. For many Buddhist paths, it is THE goal - the highest state that someone can attain, a state of enlightenment, where the mind lets go of any desire or craving.

It's a vision so powerful that it convinced the bandit Angulimala to do a total life makeover. And you know what? There's absolutely no reason why you can't do the same.

Think about life as being on a giant roller coaster. There are ups and downs, thrilling moments, and scary drops. Sometimes, you feel like you're just holding on for dear life, hoping to get through it. *Nirvana* is like stepping off that roller coaster and watching it from a bench – calm, cool, and collected. You're no longer tossed around by the highs and lows. You're just at peace, watching it all go by without letting it shake you.

As we've discussed in the previous chapters, a lot of our daily stress and pain come from our wants and dislikes. We cling to things we like (e.g. ice cream, sunny days, or compliments) and really dislike other things (e.g. getting caught in the rain without an umbrella, or someone cutting us off in traffic). We also suffer because sometimes, we just don't see things clearly. We think that permanent happiness can come from things that are actually temporary.

For example, when we think about buying a new phone, it's exciting at first, right? But that excitement fades, and soon enough, we're eyeing the next model. Or consider how we react when plans get canceled or things don't go our way. It can ruin our mood completely. This kind of suffering happens because we're attached to how we want things to be.

Achieving *nirvana* is about breaking free from these patterns. It means realizing deeply that most of what we chase (or run from) doesn't lead to lasting happiness because everything changes. That new phone becomes just another phone, and rainy days are just part of life.

Someone who reaches *nirvana* stops reacting automatically with craving or aversion. They don't get overly excited or deeply disappointed by the ups and downs of life. What they have instead is a steady kind of contentment that isn't reliant on conditions – whether they're sitting in traffic or winning the lottery, they remain at peace.

That's exactly the state I strived to be in, once I started following Buddhist principles. And it's a state I tried to maintain even when great things started happening for me. I was careful to not let myself be overcome with excitement.

You see, we often think of excitement as happiness, but as Thich Nhat Hanh points out in "The Art of Power": "Many people think excitement is happiness....But when you are excited you are not peaceful. True happiness is based on peace."

For example, once I started exploring Buddhism, I felt moved to share what I was learning with other people. I started up my own blog – Hack Spirit – about self-development and my interest in Buddhism and meditation. To my surprise, the site showed promising signs right away, and I quickly learnt that I was onto a winner here. People were enjoying what I was saying and I was getting thousands of visitors a day to my startup blog. The growing success of my blog felt like building the foundations of a house. It was a small structure, to be sure, but it was real and it was inspiring me.

But – and this is important to note – at the same time, I wasn't obsessing about it and I was certainly not having any anxiety about whether or not it would stand up in the long run. The old me would definitely not have been that calm and stoic. The old me would have been caught up in varying states of exhilaration and worrying, a jumble of nerves and restlessness.

Now, I was living my life boldly and authentically and finding that it was its own reward. Mind you, I was still in a really unsure place. By then I had left my warehouse job and accepted my brother Brendan's invitation to stay with him in Thailand. It was a thrill to be in a new place for sure, but it still carried with it a touch of uncertainty – I was far from home, and besides, I didn't even know what I considered home anymore. It felt a little like being in limbo.

But I was getting comfortable in my own skin, and I was shedding lots of the attachments and obsessive thoughts about the future that had kept me down previously. Following the Buddhist principle of *Nirodha*, I simply put in my best effort on a regular basis and let the process unfold. I chose action over agonizing, and solutions over victimhood and suffering.

You might be thinking, "That's great for enlightened monks, maybe, but what about me?"

Here's the good news: just working towards *nirvana* can seriously cut down on daily stresses and boost your happiness.

So how can you start moving towards this state of cool calm? It's actually simpler than you think:

- **Meditate**: Spend some time each day sitting quietly, focusing on your breath or the sensations in your body. This helps you get better at noticing your thoughts and feelings without getting swept away by them.
- **Reflect on impermanence**: Regularly remind yourself that everything changes. The good, the bad, and the mundane – none of it lasts

forever. This can help reduce the intensity of your reactions to life's ups and downs.

- **Cultivate compassion**: Try to understand and empathize with others. Everyone has their struggles, and often, they act out of their own unmet needs or pain. Understanding this can lessen your irritation and increase your patience and kindness.

Working towards *nirvana* isn't about detaching from life or numbing yourself to experiences. It's about engaging with life more fully, but with a wise understanding that nothing needs to shake your core peace. It's about finding joy and contentment that don't depend on life always going your way.

Wherever you are right now, whatever your own version of suffering looks like, I'm telling you, you can do the same. The state of *nirvana* is open to anyone who's willing to do the tough job of paying attention to their life and breaking the old patterns that hold them back.

The key takeaway is this:

If you have the mindset that a certain path will get you the results you want, your life becomes one of unproductive struggle.

If you leave these types of expectations behind and embrace the possibility of a different path to what you've been promised, then magic is possible.

Life isn't supposed to be easy, but it can be simple. The thing is, it's up to us to make it simple.

EXERCISE THREE
Put This Book Down

- Read this exercise and follow its instructions.
- Then put down this book.
- Lace up your shoes.
- Fill a bottle with water and grab earphones to listen to music.
- Jog for as long as you can in a safe, well-lit place for at least 30 minutes.
- Go another 15 minutes if you can.
- Hydrate well and sit in a comfortable chair and watch a ridiculous, low-brow comedy film or show.
- You can also feel free to now pick up this book and begin reading again.
- Repeat this exercise three times per week.

Note: if you can't jog for health reasons, walk. If you can't walk for health reasons, swim, stretch, or sit out in nature and watch the beauty of our natural world.

Congratulations. Exercise three is now complete.

What's the point?

Many of our biggest problems come from the suffering we heap on ourselves. The judgments, beatdowns, and hate we internally monologue and reinforce sadly often feed into a self-fulfilling prophecy.

Getting out of your head and out of emotional loops rarely happens in the head or in the emotions.

It happens in the body.

Think about it: even listening to a beautiful piece of music that somehow lifts you happens in your body, coming through one of your five senses (your ears), and penetrating into your psyche.

The above exercise is simple and its purpose is clear: to get you out of your suffering head and into your body. Mindful movement is a quick way to do that.

*

CHAPTER FOUR

Breaking Through (Magga | The Path Away From Suffering)

"No one saves us but ourselves. No one can and no one may. We ourselves must walk the path: Buddhas only show the way."

Siddharta Gautama Buddha

*O*ne day, a group of villagers gathered around the Buddha, eager to learn how to achieve peace and happiness. Among them was a man named Purna, who was particularly keen on finding a way out of his suffering. He approached the Buddha and asked, "Buddha, can you tell us the way to enlightenment? We want to follow your path and find peace."

The Buddha looked at Purna and the villagers with a kind smile. He said, "Imagine there is a man who has been away from his hometown for many years. One day, he meets someone who knows the way to his hometown and asks for directions. The person gives him clear and precise directions on how to get there."

The Buddha paused for a moment, letting the story sink in. Then he continued, "Now, just because the man has been given the directions, does it mean he has already reached his hometown?"

Purna and the villagers shook their heads. "No, Buddha," Purna replied. "The man has to follow the directions and make the journey himself to reach his hometown."

The Buddha nodded. "Exactly. I can show you the way to enlightenment, just like giving directions to the man's hometown. I can teach you the Noble Eightfold Path and how to live a life of mindfulness, compassion, and wisdom. But simply knowing the path is not enough. You must walk it yourselves. You *must put in the effort, practice, and dedication to make the journey."*

The villagers began to understand. The Buddha's teachings were like a map, but they had to take the steps themselves. Purna felt a sense of clarity. "So, Buddha, you can guide us, but it's up to us to follow the path and make the journey to enlightenment on our own?"

"Yes, Purna," the Buddha said gently. "I can show you the way, but you must walk it. Each person is responsible for their own journey. By following the path with determination and perseverance, you can find peace and happiness."

One of the things that first drew me to Buddhism was that you don't need to believe in anything supernatural. It's often seen as a religion without a god. Adopting the principles and practices of Buddhism doesn't require you to believe anything specific or to worship and please some higher power. For those of us who can't put their faith in the supernatural, Buddhism provides a refreshing form of spiritual guidance that doesn't ask you to suspend science and reason.

But make no mistake – you'll still have to do a lot of work. The path to enlightenment is not as light and breezy as it sounds.

It's kind of like signing up for a mental marathon. You wouldn't expect to just show up and breeze through a 26-mile race without any training, right?

Similarly, the Buddhist path, known as *magga*, requires commitment, practice, and a fair bit of sweat (the mental kind, mostly).

In Thailand, I had gotten into the daily rhythm of waking up, stretching, going for a run and then cooling off. I'd come home for a dip in Brendan's Airbnb pool and then write a post on Hack Spirit. Hack Spirit was doing quite well by now, and Brendan was hugely supportive, providing an invaluable outside reader's perspective on the blog and what he liked and disliked about it. The stats were starting to shoot up, and the idea of making this my full-time career and even growing a team around the site started to become feasible.

But the problem was, my five-week stay in Thailand was coming to an end, and I wasn't sure what was going to happen next. The thought of going back to the old job or of striking out into a psychology-related field in Australia didn't exactly appeal to me.

I meditated and kept my eyes focused on maintaining emotional and physical balance, day by day. My diet at this time was much healthier than it had been only a few months before. I was feeling lighter in my body, yet grounded in optimism and in my physical and mental self. I felt ready for life in a way I hadn't felt for years.

Once I was back in Melbourne, I knew in my heart that it was no longer where I should be. So, after only two weeks, I took action – I bought a one-way ticket back to Thailand.

There I was at 27, setting out on the adventure of my life. This time, I was going to do even more exploring, taking tips from my other brother Justin to go check out Vietnam and explore more of Thailand.

Long story short, I ended up moving to Vietnam for good a few months later.

The old me would have spent years thinking about maybe moving back to Asia when he had more money. Or he'd try to weigh all the pros and cons.

The new me did a reasonable amount of planning but also had an element of *carpe diem*.

I actually credit my meditative and Buddhist learning with helping me take action instead of remaining passive. Buddhism isn't about remaining in a peaceful blissed out state inside your head. It's about cutting through all the unnecessary noise and towards what's essential, allowing you to take clear action when you decide to do so.

I boarded that plane without much worry at all. What would be, would be: *que sera, sera*, as they say. I'd found a way to break through my monkey mind and my excuses.

I was putting my ideas into action and staking my future on it. If I succeeded, I'd learn tons and have many ups and downs. If I failed, I'd learn tons and have many ups and downs, too!

It was a win-win.

I was giving back to the world in the best way I knew how: by sharing my genuine life experiences on Hack Spirit. That was inherently worthwhile, because I knew from feedback and from my gut feeling that what I was doing had value for myself and others.

The fact that it was taking off as a business, and that it had required me to basically get an informal education in e-commerce and website building, was actually an added plus. What had felt like a major drag at the time actually launched me into a business model that's proven really relevant to our current high-tech times. I was excited about where it was going and how my newfound knowledge could help others. Every time I hit the keypad for a new post, I asked myself two questions:

Am I being true to myself and my experience?

Am I trying to give something of value to the world and not only for myself?

That's my life philosophy today in a nutshell. If the answer to both questions is yes, I proceed forward. I have these questions bookmarked in my mind – and I return to them when it comes to decision making.

Now, increasingly, how I look at life and the positive message I take from Buddhism and its Four Noble Truths is that escaping unnecessary suffering isn't actually about dissociating in an abstract way, or not caring anymore about what happens in life.

It's about shifting your paradigm so you can see the bigger picture.

It's about clarifying and focusing your efforts on what's really true to you, instead of what you think you should want or what your temporary impulses lead you to. Buddhism is about taking action that's focused on your purpose and giving of your gifts without wanting or expecting anything in return.

The giving is the reward.

It's absolutely about being in love with the journey more than the outcome.

However, that doesn't mean you turn down a win! Success in life allows you to give so much more and help so many more people. But in order to find that success buried inside you, you're going to need to find your breakthrough in life.

We all have several possibilities in our lives to break through to something more than what others expect for us or what the statistics say we should be. Finding your breakthrough in life is not going to happen in your mind or in waking up one morning and just feeling like a million bucks (although that's certainly a start). It's going to come from when your actions match your goals and your deeds match your thoughts.

My only caveat here is you should be very certain that what you love is also what you're good at doing! It's not always the case. But if you find that sweet spot where passion and skill intersect, you've hit the jackpot. This realization often comes after a lot of trial and error, and, yes, some soul-searching too. When you start aligning what you are deeply passionate about with what you excel at, you begin to live not just effectively, but meaningfully.

Understanding Magga: More Than Just a List

Unlike many spiritual paths that promise liberation as a distant, almost mythical realization, Buddhism lays out a clear and actionable path. This path isn't linear but a holistic approach involving moral, meditative, and wisdom practices that reinforce one another and all add up to slowly bring us to an awakening.

It's a series of steps – also known as the **Eightfold Path** – that help us refine our thoughts, actions, and attitudes to align with a more peaceful and insightful way of living. But don't be fooled by the simplicity of it being just a series of steps; it's the implementation that's a real doozy.

As the name suggests, it consists of eight different aspects:

- **Right Understanding:** have a correct understanding of the nature of reality and the path to enlightenment.

- **Right Thought:** keep your thoughts free of ill will toward either yourself or others.

- **Right Speech:** speak truthfully, kindly, and constructively.

- **Right Action:** act in ways that do not harm others.

- **Right Livelihood:** avoid making a living by exploiting or harming other people.

- **Right Effort:** work hard to improve yourself and overcome your negative qualities.

- **Right Mindfulness:** be aware of your thoughts, feelings, and actions in the present moment, without judgment.

- **Right Concentration:** develop concentration and focus through meditation to help you understand the world and yourself.

Following the principles of the Eightfold Path is what helped me make my own breakthrough. Applying Right Understanding, Thought, Speech, Effort, and all of that is precisely what led me to create Hack Spirit, which is what I consider my Right Livelihood.

In the next chapters of this book, I'll discuss the Eightfold Path in detail. But for now, let's focus on how this framework can start transforming your life even before you dive deep into each step. Think of it as a preview of what's to come if you decide to take this journey seriously.

Imagine this: You're at work, and a colleague says something that just gets under your skin. Now, you have a choice. The old you might snap back or start brewing a silent grudge.

But what if you apply the principles of **Right Speech** and **Right Thought**? You take a breath, decide not to let anger control your response, and address the issue calmly or let it go if it's not that significant. This doesn't just change that one interaction; it changes the whole vibe of your day and, gradually, of your life.

Or how about this scenario: You're thinking about switching jobs, and there's an opportunity that would pay more but doesn't align with your values (think excessive corporate greed or environmental disregard).

Here's where **Right Livelihood** comes into play. If you want to follow this Buddhist principle, you'd have to make a choice that aligns with your values. This is hard for many people, especially if the choice would mean sacrificing a higher salary. But the payoff is even bigger, even though it may be intangible – peace of mind and integrity. Believe me, choosing that over the hefty paycheck is a deeper, more sustainable type of satisfaction.

Are you beginning to see how the principles act like guideposts?

Don't get me wrong – it sounds neat when laid out like this, but it's tough in practice. Every day, every moment presents a new challenge, a new decision. That's why Buddhism is less about having a serene few minutes of morning meditation (though that's great!) and more about how you live your life from moment to moment.

So is it worth the effort? Absolutely. The benefits of this path are profound and personal. You start seeing the world more clearly, experiencing less frustration, feeling more at peace with the flow of life. You may even come to enjoy the chaos sometimes because you're no longer resisting it so much. You find clarity and maybe even joy in places where all you used to see was stress and obstacles.

As we venture into the next chapters, where I'll lay out each aspect of the Eightfold Path, keep in mind that the journey is as important as the destination. The changes you make along the way, how you refine your thoughts, choose your words, and direct your actions – it all shapes not only the path to enlightenment but the quality of your everyday life.

It's about becoming more intentional, more conscious, and, yes, more enlightened, step by step. So, while it may be a lot of work, it's also incredibly rewarding. And trust me, it's worth every step.

Ready to take that step? Let's continue this journey together and explore this path that Buddhism offers to transform your perspective and your entire life.

EXERCISE FOUR
Breakthrough

What is your biggest problem in life which is bringing you suffering and which you can't seem to overcome, no matter how hard you try and how much you improve?

Make a Word or Google Doc with this problem in all large caps.

Screenshot the document and put the image as your computer background right now.

For example:

- I hate my life in every single way
- My body causes me enormous pain
- My anxiety is so strong I feel unable to live
- I feel empty without a mission to commit to in life
- I feel like I'll always be alone
- I'm terrified of dying
- I feel completely lonely
- I have no idea how to get a decent job
- It seems like life has no purpose
- I'm worried everyone I love will disappear

You're going to see this a lot. Every time you see your laptop or computer desktop.

Reflect on it. Look at those words hard. Imagine

you're a different person feeling exactly the same way as those words.

What are you doing right now, each day, to help others who are suffering from this similar frustration in life and who also feel completely stuck?

In what way are you the solution to this problem for others?

For example, if you've written that you feel unhappy being alone, are you going out of your way to make sure others don't feel alone? Maybe you have retrained as a counselor, or you are going to open a board game café. Maybe you will create a new video game where players interact at a deeper level. Maybe you will just take some homemade chili to your lonely next-door neighbor whose husband died last year.

If you're not doing anything concrete, start now. Even if it's small, start now.

What's the point?

The best of intentions remain just that: intentions.

True commitment means actually spending time and effort (maybe even money), working, getting up and putting on a suit or a hard hat. It means actually helping others and being a difference-maker in this flawed old world we live in.

It means using your mind, heart, and hands to start becoming the one you are waiting for.

Nobody else is going to come. And everyone else who's struggling and alone right now is going to be wondering when somebody will finally just step up and do something too.

That someone is you.

Forget about overthinking it, and don't you dare dip just a toe in the water with the option not to jump in if it's too cold.

Find that burning passion inside yourself.

Your greatest victory will come at the point of your greatest frustration, and help to transform that reality for others. Once you put your thoughts and words into action for a meaningful purpose, magic happens.

PART TWO

The Eightfold Path

*

CHAPTER FIVE

Cracking the Code (Samma ditthi | Right Understanding)

"The importance of right view can be gauged from the fact that our perspectives on the crucial issues of reality and value have a bearing that goes beyond mere theoretical convictions. They govern our attitudes, our actions, our whole orientation to existence. Our views might not be clearly formulated in our mind; we might have only a hazy conceptual grasp of our beliefs. But whether formulated or not, expressed or maintained in silence, these views have a far-reaching influence. They structure our perceptions, order our values, crystallize into the ideational framework through which we interpret to ourselves the meaning of our being in the world."

Bhikkhu Bodhi, The Noble Eightfold Path:
Way to the End of Suffering

People came from far and wide to seek the Buddha's wisdom and guidance. One day, a group of villagers approached the Buddha with a dispute. They had been arguing about the nature of truth and reality, and they couldn't agree on what was true.

The Buddha, seeing their confusion, decided to teach them a lesson about "Samma Dithi," or Right Understanding. He called upon several blind men and brought them to the villagers. Then, he had an elephant brought.

He asked each of the blind men to touch a different part of the elephant and describe what they felt. One man touched the elephant's side and said, "An elephant is like a wall." Another felt the trunk and said, "No, an elephant is like a snake."

A third man touched the tusk and argued, "An elephant is like a spear." Yet another touched the leg and insisted, "An elephant is like a tree trunk." Finally, the last blind man felt the tail and claimed, "An elephant is like a rope."

The villagers listened to the blind men argue, each convinced that his perception was the correct one. The Buddha then spoke to the villagers and the blind men, "You see, each of you is only partially correct. Each of you has experienced only a part of the elephant, but none of you have seen the whole truth.

This is how many people perceive the world—they see only a part of the truth and believe it to be the whole."

The Buddha continued, "Right Understanding means seeing things as they truly are, in their entirety. It is about understanding the nature of reality, not just from one limited perspective, but from a complete and holistic view. This is the first step on the path to enlightenment."

He explained further, "To cultivate Right Understanding, one must practice wisdom and insight, seeing beyond surface appearances and comprehending the true nature of life. This includes understanding the Four Noble Truths and recognizing the impermanent, unsatisfactory, and non-self nature of all phenomena."

The villagers and the blind men began to grasp the deeper meaning of the Buddha's teaching. They realized that their arguments and disagreements stemmed from a limited and partial understanding of reality. They thanked the Buddha for his wisdom and resolved to seek a more complete and truthful understanding of life.

You can practically see the light bulb switching on in the villagers' heads in that story, right? That's exactly what happens when you gain Right Understanding – the path, the big picture, suddenly becomes clear. And you begin to see how limited your old views are.

Right Understanding involves a couple of key insights:

1. **The Four Noble Truths**: This is Buddhism 101. Understanding that life has inherent suffering, that there's a cause for this suffering, that there's an end to suffering, and there's a path that leads to this end (the Eightfold Path).
2. **Karma and Its Consequences**: Every action has a reaction. Grasping this helps us make choices that lead to positive outcomes, not just for ourselves but for others around us.
3. **Impermanence and Non-Self**: Nothing lasts forever, and the "self" we often fight so hard to protect doesn't exist in the way we think it does. This isn't meant to be bleak; it's actually liberating. It frees us from clinging to things that only cause more suffering.

This helps guide us to think, speak, act, work, try, focus, and concentrate in ways that lead to ending suffering and finding enlightenment. You can imagine it like this — it's like your inner GPS on the Noble Eightfold Path. It points you in the right direction straight from the start. It's about seeing life for what it really is — ephemeral and constantly changing. And unless we're able to cope with its unpredictable and ever changing nature, we're bound to drown in our own anguish.

Clinging to possessions, moments, or ideas is like trying to get a river to stay still. It's absolutely futile. You know the river is going to keep flowing whether you like it or not. What's the point in despairing over it?

Right Understanding helps you face life's ups and downs with a clearer mind and a more open heart. It's like calibrating your internal compass to truth, making every step you take more meaningful and a whole lot more rewarding.

Applying Right Understanding

I had been a "blind man" myself, seeing things only from one point of view that was absolutely narrow and limited. This was especially true when it came to my love life.

When I first moved to Vietnam, I had the time of my life scoping out the dating scene. I'd use apps and a couple dating sites, as well as just asking out girls I'd meet out and about. I was hoping for a relationship, but I was also open to having some fun if that was what was on the menu. I went on quite a few dates with girls who caught my eye or seemed eager to talk, but then when the attraction died down, I'd find that there just wasn't a strong connection. For want of a better word, nothing was really 'clicking.'

After only a month or two, I was dead tired of meaningless dates and encounters. At the same time, my growth in Buddhism warned me that it was important to have the right understanding (*samma ditthi*) in order to avoid unnecessary suffering.

Truth is, there's no amount of intimacy or physical pleasure that can ever satisfy us, although people like Hugh Hefner may have tried to test that principle out to the max.

It's also important in Buddhism to exercise self-control. Gluttonous eating, casual sex, and drinking and drugs are all discouraged because they are ways we can often get more addicted and attached to life's fleeting pleasures.

I realized I'd been looking at finding love a little bit like a prize or a jackpot. A gift from the universe that would "complete" me, and bring me inner peace and harmony.

Just as my work life hadn't really come together until I'd started generating my own authentic actions connected to my goals, my love life only began coming together when I stopped lying to myself. I racked my brain and thought about the subject and realized that if I never gave myself time to truly be alone, and kept trying to run from this feeling of not having a partner, I could end up living my whole life in a self-fulfilling cycle.

I began being much more selective and dating only when and who I wanted to. I began to hang back more and focus on writing and the website. I became truly comfortable with being alone. I let it be.

And some months later, this process of allowing solitude to take its course and restore me to a kind of patience and self-control really worked its magic.

This first step of the Eightfold Path isn't easy, even though many of us think it is. Understanding the roots of suffering, and learning to get out of our own way, requires us to sometimes go against conventional wisdom.

Besides, who said conventionality is the way to be anyway?

We all need to have this gear shift.

Your life is yours to design – and you can be as creative as you like, so don't deprive yourself of opportunities and settle for something second-rate.

You get to decide what first-rate looks like.

If you're ready to be radically honest with yourself, start with looking closely at your motivations, fears, and hopes. Knowing these philosophical concepts is one thing, but putting them into action is where the real magic happens. Here's how you can start applying Right Understanding in your day-to-day life:

1. **Reflect on Your Experiences**: Take time each day to reflect on the impermanence and outcomes of your actions. Did something upset you today? Consider how your attachment to a certain outcome might have contributed to your distress.

2. **Mindful Decision-Making**: Use your understanding of karma to guide your decisions. Ask yourself, "What are the potential consequences of this action? Is it beneficial? Is it harmful?" Making this kind of questioning a habit can transform your actions and their impacts.

Remember: We are constantly evolving, and nothing is ever set in stone! You can be a totally different person tomorrow from who you are today.

EXERCISE FIVE
Kaleidoscope Views

- Write down the reasons your last relationship or dating endeavors failed to the best of your knowledge.
- Write down what you *think* the other individual would write as the reason that this relationship or date failed.
- Write down what your best friend would probably think about why this relationship failed.
- Write down what your worst enemy would probably think about why it failed.
- Look at these varying points of view.
- Who is most correct and why? How can you know for sure?
- You can also use this exercise for other areas of your life, like your career or an event that has affected you in a huge way.

What's the point?

Getting a mental grip is about being honest on how many ways there are to look at the same situation.

Once you see how subjective the understanding of a social situation can be, you can begin to grapple with *right understanding* in a meaningful way.

Start by admitting you don't understand and that despite trying to the best of your ability, many things have confused you and left you baffled.

Let that simmer.

Meditate on not understanding fully what's going on and why. Being lost is good. It's a hell of a lot better than sprinting in the wrong direction or pretending you know where you are.

Sink into this lost feeling and make friends with it.

I will build on this later.

*

CHAPTER SIX

Curating the Mind (Samma sankappa | Right Thoughts)

"All that we are is the result of what we have thought: it is founded on our thoughts, it is made up of our thoughts. If a man speaks or acts with a pure thought, happiness follows him, like a shadow that never leaves him."

Siddharta Gautama Buddha

Tthere's a lot out there these days about positive thinking, the Law of Attraction, and so on. Buddhism has also become stereotyped as being about "going with the flow" and "thinking positive."

There's definitely an element of flow in Buddhist practices. But before I go any further, take a second to think about your preconceptions of Buddhism and what you really think it's about.

You see, it's not really about being "positive" or trying your best to be happy. It's about being realistic, and accepting reality. It's also about noticing your thoughts without identifying and believing in all of them.

The idea that you can "create" and manifest your reality is partly correct. Our thoughts and values begin to shape the lenses through which we see the world.

But the idea that a person in a car accident drew that event towards themselves through negative energy, as spiritual teachers like Eckhart Tolle claim, is silly nonsense.

That's my perspective, at least.

Yes, Buddhism is about finding inner peace, letting go of the need to stroke your ego and find fulfillment in external things.

Yes, it's about cultivating love and care for all beings.

But it does not mean you dream in rainbow colors on the back of a unicorn while shimmery exotic music plays. This does not necessarily mean you try to consciously only form positive or "high vibration" thoughts, as some Buddhist books may teach.

We often don't have a choice about the suffering and surprises that life throws our way. Pretending we'll be fine by putting on a brave face is foolish. Rejecting or repressing angry, sad, confused, and other "negative" thoughts leads us to a very false and disempowered place in life.

We need the rain just as much as we need the sun.

The Elements of Right Intention

We all have negative and self-defeating thoughts. Our subconscious is a powerful machine. Thoughts arise and pass away. Having right thoughts or intentions (*samma sankappa*) is about choosing which thoughts to pursue, rather than cultivating thoughts intentionally.

Our conscious self chooses to identify or not identify with them. It might be only a split microsecond in which we decide which to identify with, but it most certainly is a choice, no matter how ingrained it has become. That's where our power is: in choosing which thoughts to identify and having a reason to do so.

Now, how do you do that? It's pretty simple, actually. You just need to make sure that your thoughts have the key parts of Right Intention:

- **Intentions of Renunciation (*Nekkhamma*)**: This means letting go of harmful desires and attachments. Think of it like deciding not to plant weeds in your garden. By avoiding things that can cause suffering or trouble, you make space for healthier, more positive things to grow.

- **Intentions of Goodwill (*Avyapada*)**: This is about wanting good things for yourself and others. It's like planting flowers that bring beauty and joy to everyone who sees them. When you have kind and compassionate thoughts, you're more likely to do kind and compassionate things.

- **Intentions of Harmlessness (*Ahimsa*)**: This means not wanting to harm others. Imagine planting a tree that provides shade and fruit without hurting anything around it. By avoiding thoughts of anger or harm, you contribute to a more peaceful and happy environment.

Essentially, you want to encourage the thoughts that come to you which encourage *nekkhamma*, *avyapada*, and *ahimsa*.

You'll have plenty that don't! That's part of life. Remember, you won't magically turn into someone who only has pure thoughts all the time.

So don't force a smile and say you've never wanted to punch someone in the face – repressing anger will just turn you fake. Instead, accept and transform your selfishness (deeply tied to fear of inadequacy and abandonment).

Accept and transform your desire to defeat others or take advantage of them (tied to fear of losing control or being hurt).

Accept and transform your desire to harm other creatures (linked to instinctual urges of competition for mates and fear of death).

These are all part of us. But the thoughts that come to us saying that we must give in to these instincts are lying. We can choose to pursue the thoughts that help us begin to transform these impulses.

A few months after I moved to Vietnam, I started exploring the Buddhist communities there. I reached out to one near me, and I quickly became fast friends with Diep, a 42-year-old baker.

Now Diep was not by any measure a rich guy; his bakery was a very modest one, located in a narrow, bustling street that often smelled of fresh bread and exhaust fumes. Despite his humble circumstances, though, he always walked around with a smile, and his little shop was a haven of warmth and delicious aromas.

As I got to know him better, Diep shared that his contentment didn't come from what he owned or his financial status, but from his mindset and the way he thought about life. He shared with me that embracing Right Thought was a vital part of his daily practice.

"We all have the ability to choose how we are in the world and how we deal with our emotions," he explained.

And it's true. We can choose to not sit with negative emotions and dwell in our pain. We can choose to not act on impulse, and to instead pause and see the bigger picture.

Most importantly, we can choose to steer our minds away from the three poisons of greed, ill will, and delusion, which are often the root causes of suffering.

It's all a matter of *choice*.

Diep's example was particularly striking when it came to dealing with competition. A new bakery had opened right across the street, one with modern decor and an extensive advertising budget. I asked him if he was worried about losing customers.

"Of course, I noticed the new bakery," Diep said, chuckling softly. "It's hard not to see it when I open up every morning. But in Buddhism, we learn to practice right thought by wishing others well, even our competitors. Instead of harboring jealousy or fear, I focus on making the best bread I can and treating every customer who walks into my shop with kindness and respect."

Diep's approach was to view the situation not as a threat, but as an opportunity to reaffirm his values and commitment to his craft. "If my neighbor does well, that's good for him. If I do well, that's good for me. And if we both do well, that's good for our community," he added.

Well, I was just blown away by his goodness of heart. I wasn't sure I could be that full of goodwill myself! But it's such a great example of how Right Thought can free us from anxiety and negativity and allow us to go on doing good work.

In Diep's case, he could go on keeping his customers happy and his shop thriving despite the competition. He made it a point to regularly meditate and reflect on his thoughts, so that they would always be aligned with the principles of goodwill and harmlessness.

As Diep's friend, I learned an invaluable lesson about the practical application of Right Thought. It wasn't just about avoiding negative thoughts, but actively transforming them into positive intentions that guide your actions. This approach didn't just make Diep a better businessman – it made him a happier and more fulfilled person.

So, whenever you find yourself facing challenges, whether in personal relationships, business, or any other aspect of life, remember Diep's bakery across from its flashy competitor. Think about how applying Right Thought – choosing thoughts of kindness, non-harm, and generosity – can not only change your internal state but can also positively affect your surroundings and the people in it.

EXERCISE SIX
Brain Freeze

Let's face it, we're often more selfish than we care to admit. It's precisely our selfish nature that causes us to cling to things. This exercise is designed to help you shift mindsets and act out of kindness.

Every single day for the next week, do the following:

- One entirely unselfish act that you wouldn't normally do in order to help someone from whom you gain absolutely nothing by helping them, not even their thanks or any outer recognition.
- Shut down and "freeze" your regular brain that would usually tell you why bother or that you don't have enough time or money or energy to help.
- Freeze your me-first brain that wants to know what's in it for you or notices whether a person you help is physically attractive, rich or poor, or any other attributes of them apart from them needing help in some way!
- Preferably, help someone anonymously or in a way they aren't even aware it was you who helped. Just help because you can.
- If you don't have any possible way to help someone right now, make an online donation to a worthy cause you believe in every day, even if it's only $1 a day.

What's the point?

Throughout his life, the Buddha emphasized the importance of giving to others, not harming others, and having good intentions toward others – even those you personally dislike or find disagreeable.

Helping is something that society often encourages, but it is often infected by bragging and moral virtue signaling.

"Hey, look at me, I support popular cause ABC, and so on! I donated money and changed the frame on my profile pic!"

This is not the way.

Instead, make helping someone a part of your daily life, even if it's in small ways. Do it out of the public eye as much as possible. Try helping and not even telling anyone you did it. Try seeking zero recognition or even wanting thanks, but just helping because you can.

If you like it a lot, you could continue even longer than after one week, or as long as you can. Hopefully, helping others will become a natural thing you do, and that's a sign that you're learning how to pursue Right Thought.

*

CHAPTER SEVEN

The Power of Words
(Samma vaca | Right Speech)

"Better than a thousand hollow words, is one word that brings peace."

Siddharta Gautama Buddha

One sunny afternoon, I found myself in a crowded café in Saigon, headphones in, trying to focus on my work. But no amount of lo-fi beats could drown out the rising voices at the table next to mine.

A young couple was arguing, their voices getting more and more angry and frustrated. The café's ambient noise seemed to fade into the background as their dispute grew louder. Then, suddenly, the man said something — a sharp, cutting remark about the woman's family. The words hung heavy in the air, and the immediate silence that followed was deafening. The woman's face crumbled; she stood up and left, tears streaming down her face. The man sat back, his anger dissolving into a look of regret.

This moment stuck with me — that brief exchange highlighted the power of words to hurt, to heal, to destroy, and to mend. It was a stark reminder of why Right Speech, or Samma Vaca, is a crucial aspect of the Buddhist Eightfold Path.

With right understanding and thoughts, right speech is often the byproduct. It's something we should all be highly conscious of as humans.

Because the truth is that trash talk and loose lips sink ships like:

- Relationships
- Friendships
- Business partnerships

When we lie about others, say hateful things about them and spread rumors, we make the world a worse place.

Let's face it:

Some people basically do it for entertainment, and it seems like half of what's on TV these days is, more or less, extended gossip and drama sessions on reality TV. There's certainly a market for it. But, at the end of the day, it's exhausting and vacuous crap that won't do you any good in your life.

I've always considered right speech to be directly related to my writing. I write what I've experienced and what I believe. I don't write what I "should" or what is popular. I'm interested in what's really true, not just stuff that feels good to hear but doesn't really mean anything or isn't realistic.

For that reason, I care a lot about what I say and why. Not only do I have the potential to influence many people and help them change their lives, I have the potential to implant self-limiting doubts, toxic views, or bad habits in readers if I give stupid advice.

What Makes Up Right Speech?

In Buddhism, Right Speech isn't just about avoiding falsehood. It's so much more than that — it's about speaking truthfully, yes, but also kindly, helpfully, and harmoniously. It's about using our words to create better connections with others, to soothe instead of scratch, to build rather than break down.

Practicing Right Speech means making a conscious effort to think before you speak, to consider not just what you want to say, but how it will be received. It's about striving to ensure that your words always reflect your intentions, which should always be rooted in goodwill.

If you want to develop Right Speech, then here are four key aspects to consider:

- **Truthfulness**: Always speak the truth. This sounds straightforward, but it's more than just avoiding lies. It also involves being honest about one's thoughts, feelings, and beliefs, not only with others but also with oneself.
- **Harmonious Speech**: This aspect of Right Speech focuses on avoiding words that create discord among people. Does it have shades of gossip? Backbiting? If it has the potential to hurt someone, it isn't harmonious speech.
- **Gentle Speech**: Using gentle speech means refraining from harsh words, insults, or sarcasm. Think about how saying something in a moment of anger can lead to regret. Even in heated moments, remember to be mindful of what you say.
- **Meaningful Speech**: Engaging in meaningful speech involves avoiding idle chatter, which

can often prove challenging, especially in social situations. The goal here is to ensure that your words are impactful, purposeful, and add value to the conversation.

Practicing Right Speech is not without its challenges. I've found myself in situations where it's tempting to join in on a juicy piece of gossip or to snap back with a witty but cutting remark. It's human to feel these impulses, but Buddhism teaches us to notice these impulses and choose a different path.

One strategy that has helped me immensely is bringing **mindfulness** into my conversations. It's all about really tuning in to what the other person is saying, not just nodding along while you mentally rehearse what you're going to throw back at them. It's about ditching the mental multitasking and being totally there, in that moment, with that person. When you do this, you really start to grasp the weight of your words and how they land on others, which lets you tweak your tone and timing to make sure you're coming across as kind and thoughtful.

Another helpful practice has been **reflective listening,** which honestly, has smoothed over more rough patches than I can count. It's pretty straightforward: you just echo back what someone has told you, but in your own words. It sounds simple, but it's super effective. It shows you're paying attention and actually care about what they're saying, which can make the other person feel valued and understood. Plus, it's a great way to make sure you've got the right end of the stick before you respond, which can save a lot of headaches and heartaches down the line. This little trick can really bridge the gap when things are getting tense and make sure everyone's on the same page.

The point is this:

Be conscious of what you say and why. In general, speak less and listen more. You'll be surprised how much you learn, even when others don't say much.

Words are powerful. They can start wars or broker peace; they can wound deeply or heal profoundly. Make the latter your goal.

EXERCISE SEVEN
Watch Your Mouth

- For an entire week, don't say anything that's motivated by jealousy, hate, anger, sadness, exhaustion, or desire for egotistical satisfaction or being proven correct.

- This includes bragging around dates, showing off on social media, criticizing individuals, speaking out against public figures or groups you dislike, and so on.

- You can think it (try not to identify though, as we discussed in right thought), but *don't say it!*

- At the end of this week, even unkind comments about a meal you disliked or the weather should be nowhere to be found.

- Even if you're screaming it inside your head ("this macaroni tastes like fucking recycled barf!"), *do not say it!*

- After the week is up, write down a paragraph about how you feel.

- Write down if anything has changed in how others react to you and treat you in a general sense.

What's the point?

Samma vaca is hard! I didn't realize how often I say negative and downer things to other people and to myself until I stopped doing it as much.

It turns out I'd gotten so used to complaining and verbalizing what was wrong that it had actually become a habit, slowly feeding into an energy-lowering cycle.

Here's the thing: once you start paying attention to your speech, you really begin to notice patterns. And breaking those patterns? Well, that's where the challenge lies, but also where the growth happens. Let's face it, shifting from a habit of negative speaking to one that's more positive isn't just about biting your tongue. It's about changing your mindset.

So, get into the habit of actively listening to the words you're using. Are they positive? Are they helpful? Are they necessary? When you catch yourself slipping into old habits of negativity, pause and reframe your thoughts. Find something constructive or kind to say. Or if that's too hard, just smile. You might be surprised at how effective this can be at turning things around.

Over time, you'll likely notice a significant shift in your interactions and your overall sense of wellbeing. Practicing Right Speech isn't just about following a rule; it's about creating a more positive, mindful way of interacting with the world.

CHAPTER EIGHT

Purposeful Living (Samma kammanta | Right Action)

"Ceasing to do evil, learning to do good, purifying the heart — this is the teaching of the Buddhas."

Siddharta Gautama Buddha

Remember the story of the bandit Angulimala? After a deeper conversation with the Buddha, where he learned about peace and the consequences of his actions, he had a complete change of heart. He threw away his weapons, vowed to follow the Buddha, and became a monk. Despite facing ongoing suspicion and hostility from those he had wronged, Angulimala committed to his new path of non-violence and eventually achieved enlightenment.

I was so impressed when I first heard this story. It's dramatic for sure, like a Hollywood movie with a good redemption arc. But more than that, it highlights a core principle in Buddhism and other Eastern philosophies – the power of transformation and the importance of *ahimsa*, or non-harm. This principle is at the heart of Right Action.

Ahimsa

Ahimsa, or the principle of non-harm, is a central concept in Buddhism that has always resonated deeply with me. Basically, it teaches us to avoid causing pain to any living being, whether human, animal, or plant.

I mean, obviously, we know that we should avoid doing acts of violence, right? But are we as careful in causing no harm to any living being, whether intentionally or unintentionally? Before I learned about Buddhism, I certainly wasn't very mindful of my actions – I did what I wanted to do, often without considering if it would hurt other people.

This principle can really change the way you interact with the world. It will challenge you to consider how you can live more compassionately and mindfully. Think about it this way: every action, every decision we make has ripples. Choosing *ahimsa* means being mindful of those ripples, whether you're deciding what to eat, how to commute, or how to react in stressful situations. It's about more than just not hurting someone; it's about actively cultivating kindness and consideration.

Let me share a personal story to put this into perspective. A few years back, I was involved in a minor car accident. It was a stressful moment, and both of us could have easily lost our tempers. (The old me probably would have.) Fortunately, I was already into Buddhism by then, and remembering the principle of *ahimsa*, I took a deep breath and calmly approached the other driver. We checked if everyone was okay before worrying about the vehicles. That small act of ensuring safety over property not only helped in keeping the situation calm but also opened up a space for compassionate interaction between us. We ended up handling the situation much more amicably than if we had let our initial reactions take control.

This experience was a practical application of *ahimsa* in daily life. It showed me that non-harm isn't passive; it's an active choice that sometimes requires you to go against your instincts or immediate emotions. It's about pausing, reflecting, and choosing the path that minimizes harm.

In the broader sense, *ahimsa* is the reason for the lifestyle choices of many Buddhists. For instance, many I know have switched to vegetarian or even vegan diets. It's not just because they're chasing some health trend. It's deeper than that – it's about respect for all life forms. They just don't feel right about causing pain to other beings.

When you start seeing every creature, big and small, as deserving respect and kindness, it kind of naturally shifts how you act. Your everyday choices start to line up with those values. It's about doing no harm, not just because it sounds nice, but because it feels right deep down.

"We human beings have always singled ourselves out from the rest of the natural world. We classify other animals and living beings as 'Nature,' a thing apart from us, and act as if we're somehow separate from it. Then we ask, 'How should we deal with Nature?' We should deal with Nature the way we should deal with ourselves: nonviolently. Human beings and Nature

are inseparable. Just as we should not harm ourselves, we should not harm Nature."

- ***Thich Nhat Hanh, Nature and Nonviolence***

"Every living being deserves to enjoy a sense of security and well-being. We should protect life and bring happiness to others. All living beings, whether large or small; whether two-legged or four-legged; whether swimmers or fliers, have a right to live."

- ***The Buddha, as quoted in Thich Nhat Hanh, Path of Compassion***

Ahimsa also isn't just about how we treat others; it's also about how we treat ourselves. Sometimes, in our rush to be kind to everyone else, we totally forget about being kind to ourselves. Skipping out on self-care? That's actually a form of harm too. Practicing ahimsa means catching yourself when you're being way too tough on yourself and giving yourself a break, the same kind of break you'd give to others.

And another thing – it's not just something you do alone – it's a big-picture kind of deal. It starts with the little choices we make every day but can ripple out to really change whole communities and societies. When we pick non-harm as our default setting, we're adding to a culture of peace and kindness, which, let's be honest, the world could really use a lot more of right now.

So, it could be as simple as letting that spider chill in your home instead of freaking out, choosing a veggie burger over beef, or staying chill and caring in the middle of an argument. Ahimsa fits into every part of life, nudging us to really think about the impact of our actions and always to pick the kindest route, not just for us but for everyone around. That's a pretty amazing way to spread some good vibes in the world, don't you think?

How will ahimsa manifest in your life?

Well, the first step is to reduce the harm you cause to yourself. Negative self talk, guilt, and anger are all subtle acts of violence that affect our state of mind.

- Forgive yourself for your own mistakes and let them go.
- Moderate your expectations of yourself and don't scold yourself with negative thoughts if you fail to meet those expectations.
- Congratulate yourself on the things you've achieved and appreciate your own skills and talents.
- Take time to rest when you need it.
- Eat healthy and nutritious food.
- Accept the limitations of your own body and don't use force or inflict physical pain on

yourself when you perform yoga or other exercises.

As discussed above, it's also important to reduce the harm you cause to others. Harboring negative or unkind thoughts is bad for your own mental health and the people around you.

- Let go of your anger and irritation with the people around you; remember they are struggling just as you are.
- Resist the urge to throw insults at people, or to retaliate when they do it to you.
- Don't spread negative gossip about others and concentrate on their positive qualities.
- Nurture an attitude of loving kindness towards everyone you meet.

Finally, you need to reduce the harm you cause to the world. Whenever we give in to consumer culture and buy things we don't need, the brief pleasure we get is outweighed by the guilt we often feel for harming the environment or not giving enough to charity. The teachings of Buddhism are about rejecting that superficial pleasure in favor of the deeper happiness that comes from valuing the world around you.

- Reduce the amount you buy and instead focus on the things you already own that bring you joy.
- Buy things secondhand and give away or recycle things instead of throwing them in the trash.
- Get solar panels for your house or switch to a hybrid car to reduce your impact on the environment.
- Adopt a vegetarian diet or cut back on the amount of meat you eat, which reduces your carbon footprint as well as the harm done to animals.
- Adopt a pet from a rescue center – pets are great for reducing stress and encouraging social interaction.

Remember, reducing harm is first of all about reducing harm to yourself. Letting go of the burdens of guilt and anger and living more in harmony with your environment will make you feel mentally 'lighter', calmer, and happier.

The Five Precepts

When they first encounter Buddhism, many people who come from Western cultures that are heavily influenced by religions like Christianity and Islam can feel as though Buddhism lacks ethical teaching. After all, Buddhists are not commanded to wear particular clothes, eat certain foods, or keep particular days as holy days. (Many of them choose to anyway.) There's no central authority that decides how Buddhism should be practiced.

But that doesn't mean Buddhism lacks moral teaching.

In fact, when I first became interested in Buddhism, one of the ideas that really blew my mind was that all things are connected and ultimately manifestations of a single universal energy. That when we harm other beings, we ultimately harm ourselves. And by the same token, harming ourselves is harming the rest of the universe, too.

Much of Buddhist morality is built around what is known as the **Five Precepts**. This is the basic code of ethics suggested for Buddhists to follow.

They are:

- Don't kill
- Don't steal
- Don't engage in sexual misconduct including adultery, harassment, sexual assault, or sexual exploitation
- Don't lie
- Don't overindulge in intoxicants

In some ways, these resemble the Jewish and Christian 10 Commandments. However, it's interesting to notice that they are Precepts, not

Commandments. In other words, they are guides to living an ethical life, but there isn't the same obligation to follow them that there is in other religions.

But these are good rules for doing the Right Action and living a moral life. Practicing the Buddhist principles of compassion and lovingkindness means going beyond the Five Precepts and examining your behavior to determine whether you are acting from a place of enlightenment or not.

Karma

Even people who aren't too familiar with Buddhism have probably heard about *karma*. It's one of those concepts that has traveled far and wide, but like a lot of things that get popular, the version most people know isn't exactly what it's meant to be.

A lot of people think of *karma* as this cosmic justice system – like the universe's way of balancing things out. You know, what goes around comes around. Some even imagine *karma* as a sort of superhero that punishes the bad and rewards the good. But when you look at Buddhism's first Noble Truth – that life is full of suffering – this idea of *karma* as a cosmic scorekeeper doesn't really hold up.

In reality, *karma* is a Sanskrit word that means "action" or "doing." In the Buddhist view, *karma* is all about the actions we take and the effects they have, not just in this life but potentially in future lives too, if you're on board with the idea of reincarnation. But even if you don't buy into that, you can't deny that our actions have consequences, both good and bad.

Here's the deal: *karma* comes from our desires and attachments. According to Buddhism, everything that happens has a cause, and those causes lead to effects. It's like planting seeds – plant barley and you get barley, not corn.

So, if you act with good intentions, you're likely to see good results. Act poorly, and well, you get the picture. And there's no almighty power managing this; it's just a natural process, like rain falling from the sky. Plus, *karma* is personal. We each deal with the results of our own actions. No one else, not even the Buddha, can change your karma for you.

So, what does this mean for you? Well, thinking about *karma* can really change how you approach life and lead you towards making the right actions. It's a heads-up to consider the outcomes of your actions before you jump into anything. Instead of reacting out of anger or jealousy, which can lead to more trouble, *karma* nudges us to think about the bigger picture. It reminds us that when we hurt others, we're really just hurting ourselves.

So next time you're about to snap at someone or make a rash decision, pause and think about the *karma* you'll be creating. It might just help you steer towards a better course of action.

Before I end this chapter, I'd like to share a list of questions. These are questions to ask yourself so you can really zero in on your values and behavior with an eagle eye and see what needs to change.

- What are my core values, and how do they align with my actions?
- How do I make ethical decisions, and what guides my moral compass?
- In what areas of my life do I feel I compromise my values?
- How can I align my behavior more closely with principles of right action and intention?

Be honest with your answers – the whole point of this is to come face to face with whatever inconsistencies might be lurking between your ideals and your actions. Right Action isn't just about doing the right thing on the outside; it's deeply tied to who we are on the inside.

This isn't about beating yourself up. It's about getting real with yourself so you can make changes that truly reflect who you want to be.

EXERCISE EIGHT
Tuning Out

- Take a week away from all media that glorifies violence, casual sex, drug use, and sadism.
- Install an ad blocker and pop-up blocker for your computer and devices.
- Don't click the gory or sexy links or give any time to gossip and endless drama of the sexual or violent variety.
- Just let them be; they'll be there next week.
- During this week, try to watch one film, read one book, or even look every day at one piece of art or listen to one piece of music daily which holds a deeply meaningful message about life and ethics.
- Ensure that any violence, sex, or cruelty in the film, book, or artwork is only in the service of illustrating its moral point, for example the 2013 film *Railway Man* about revenge and forgiveness, or the 2008 film *Gran Torino* about racism and human transformation.
- How do you feel at the end of this week?

What's the point?

What does morality mean to you?

Is it just constraints put on you from outside, or is there a deeper core to it?

In Buddhism, morality isn't relative. It has a purpose in that it is intended to help us cease our unnecessary suffering and reach our potential as powerful beings who can help ourselves and help others.

Modern pop culture's celebration of many forms of sex, substance abuse, violence, and drama or provocative activities and subjects that are 'fun' or 'cool' or 'controversial' goes against Buddhism, much as I'd love to tell everyone to just chill.

If you find yourself feeling lost again to worldly influences, go back to your answers to the set of questions I posed earlier in this chapter. Touch base with yourself regularly and do an evaluation if your actions always align with your values.

*

CHAPTER NINE

Discover Your Calling (Samma ajiva | Right Livelihood)

"Your work is to discover your work and then with all your heart to give yourself to it."

Siddharta Gautama Buddha

O n another visit to my brother Brendan in Chiang Mai, I discovered one of my favorite philosophers: Zen master Alan Watts. A fellow Aussie writer introduced me to his work, and I was immediately inspired. Among Watts' many uplifting messages, one stood out for me: *"It is better to have a short life that is full of what you like doing, than a long life spent in a miserable way."* This wasn't the stereotypical Zen detachment but a call to live fully without overanalyzing.

My life started happening when I stopped obsessing over control and focused on the present. The more I let go, the more came to me. With my budding website, I saw the fruits of surrendering control and following my bliss.

Of course, not all was smooth sailing. Building a website, much like following a path of personal discovery, came with its own set of challenges. Even with user-friendly tools, I faced technical troubles like server downtimes and confusing plugin conflicts that seemed to pop up from nowhere. Each issue was a puzzle that required patience and a learning curve or the occasional help from my more tech-savvy friends.

Content creation was another mountain to climb. I can't say I always had the right words pouring out of me every single day. Some days, writer's block loomed large, and other times, the message I wanted to share didn't resonate as I'd hoped. I learned it was all about trial and error, figuring out what clicked with my audience and how to articulate complex ideas in engaging ways.

Balancing these elements and more was overwhelming at times. It forced me to set realistic goals and learn the art of prioritization, sometimes letting the smaller imperfections slide to focus on what really mattered.

But through all of these issues, I felt at peace. Why? Because I knew I was sticking to the principles of Right Livelihood, or *samma ajiva*.

Doing work that's true to your values

In ancient China, there was a monk who traveled from village to village teaching the Dharma and living solely on alms. One day, a wealthy merchant decided to test the monk's integrity and adherence to the Buddhist precepts, which include Right Livelihood by avoiding actions that cause harm and suffering to others.

The merchant approached the monk with a proposal, saying, "I am impressed by your teachings and your way of life. I want to offer you a bag of rice every month so that you do not need to worry about food. In return, I only ask that you keep my generosity a secret and do not tell others where the rice comes from."

The monk paused and reflected on the merchant's

offer. He realized that accepting this deal might lead him to deceive others and create a situation where his livelihood depended on withholding truth, which could breed suspicion and division among his followers.

He replied, "Thank you for your generous offer. However, I must decline. My practice requires me to live in truth and openness. Accepting your offer under a condition of secrecy would compromise the integrity of my teachings and my livelihood as a monk."

The merchant was taken aback but came to respect the monk even more for his unwavering commitment to ethical principles, even at the expense of his comfort.

Right Livelihood (*samma ajiva*) is a key part of the Buddhist path. It's about earning a living in a way that doesn't cause harm and aligns with ethical principles. The Buddha advised against certain types of work that harms others and the environment. Some examples I can easily think of are: trading in weapons, human beings, animals for slaughter, intoxicants, and poisons.

In today's world, where making money often feels like the top priority, practicing Right Livelihood can be challenging. In fact, I'd say that out of all the principles, this could be one of the toughest to actually implement. It's harder than it seems, given the modern corporate world. Many careers contribute indirectly to these harmful things.

For instance, sweatshops produce tons of clothes (also known as "fast fashion"), and people invest in mutual funds that support defense contracting. Even being a merchandiser for energy drinks, which can cause health issues, raises ethical questions.

Many jobs have complex supply chains and practices that might not align with your ethical principles. For example, working for a company that exploits labor, produces harmful products, or damages the environment can conflict with Right Livelihood.

We're all part of this system in some way, and none of us are completely clean. After all, not all of us have the luxury to be choosy about the kind of work we do. Some of us are pressed to take on jobs we don't feel good about simply because we have bills to pay and we need to eat.

However, if your work is making you feel like you're a bad person — maybe look into other options. Nothing could be worth that level of self-degradation. And you know what? The fact that you can even feel it, that you can even have that sense that you're in a bad place...that should tell you that your work doesn't align with your thoughts and values.

If you can, find a job that makes the world a better place, even if it's just on a small scale. Although it might feel like your efforts are insignificant – given how many people there are in the world – if we all did something positive on a small-scale, it would amount to a massive impact. Never underestimate your power and the influence you can have through your work. You never know who you could inspire and help through your work and what you do.

Living with Right Livelihood doesn't mean we should all become monks or leave the modern world behind us. Instead, it calls for mindfulness in our career choices. Think about what you really care about and how you can make the world a better place.

These were my thoughts when starting Hack Spirit. By being authentic, supporting others, and contributing positively, the site has grown beyond my wildest dreams. (It's also how I met my wife, but that's a story for another chapter…)

Changing your job can sometimes mean turning your life upside down. And I know as much as anyone how difficult it can be to leave even a job you're unhappy with. I know exactly how scary it feels when you're stepping away from something familiar, even if it isn't exactly good for you.

So let's make the process a little less painful:

- Take out your journal.
- Write down a list of jobs that you could do that wouldn't harm others.
- Now write down a list of jobs that you could do that would help other people. Professions like healthcare, education, social work, or the arts offer chances to practice Right Livelihood by contributing positively to society, but

you're definitely welcome to list anything else that feels helpful to you.

- Pick your favourite.
- Now, write down everything that stands between you and that job.
- Write down everything you would need to do to overcome those obstacles.

Reflecting like this can lead to more fulfilling and meaningful work. It might involve tough choices, like leaving a high-paying job that conflicts with your values or pursuing a less lucrative career that aligns more closely with non-harm and compassion. These decisions are personal and require courage and commitment.

EXERCISE NINE
Finding Your Calling

I realize it's not always possible to make the leap and change jobs just like that — especially if your job is supporting you and your family. Changing jobs is always a risk and not all of us are gamblers.

The good news is, you can still put in effort in your current job to maximize your positive impact on other people.

Here's an exercise to help you map that out.

Step 1: Reflect on Your Job

Think about your current job. Ask yourself:

- Does my work harm others or the environment?
- Does it align with my personal values?
- How does it benefit others?

Write down your thoughts.

Step 2: Make Positive Changes

Identify any parts of your job that might go against ethical principles. Think of ways to make your job more ethical, such as:

- Advocating for better practices at work
- Finding ways your role can positively impact society

- Making the most out of your interactions with colleagues
- Reducing harm in your daily tasks

List a few practical changes you can make.

Step 3: Take Action and Reflect

Choose one change and start working on it. After a month, reflect on:

- How do you feel about this change?
- What challenges did you face?
- What are the next steps?

Write down your reflections.

What's the point?

Most of us spend a huge chunk of our waking hours at work. It's a massive part of our lives, but let's be honest, not all of us are in our dream jobs. And even if we are, there are always parts of our jobs that could use a little ethical sprucing up.

This exercise is your chance to take a step back and really look at what you do through a different lens – not just in terms of paycheck or career progression but in terms of impact.

Mapping out how your job impacts others and brainstorming ways to tweak things for the better can help you make the best of your work situation, especially if it isn't an ideal one.

This isn't just about feeling good about yourself (though that's a pretty nice perk). It's about making sure that how you make a living doesn't just fill your pockets but also does good in the world – or at least doesn't cause harm.

And here's the kicker: when you start making these changes, you might just find that your job satisfaction starts to climb. Knowing that your work is more in tune with your values can make the daily grind a lot less…grindy. Plus, advocating for better practices or finding new ways to bring positive impacts can seriously boost your sense of agency and purpose.

*

CHAPTER TEN

A Good Day's Work
(Samma vayama | Right Effort)

"The Fourfold Right Diligence is nourished by joy and interest. If your practice does not bring you joy, you are not practicing correctly."

Thich Nhat Hahn

To really advance along the Buddha's Noble Eightfold Path and in life in general, you've got to put in the effort. Progress won't just land in your lap; you have to actively pursue it and practice it.

But it's also important to remember that while diligence is key, it's also about smart effort – not just grinding for the sake of grinding. You have to find the right balance that keeps you motivated without burning out.

How do you do that? By setting realistic goals, understanding your limits, and also knowing when to take a step back and recharge.

The path really is an exercise in consistency and perseverance – *filling a jug drop by drop*, as the Buddha said. But it also demands awareness of how we're directing our energies. Working smart on the Eightfold Path means tuning into yourself, understanding your mental and emotional thresholds, and adjusting your efforts accordingly. It's about recognizing when your practices are genuinely beneficial and when they might just be ticking boxes. This discernment is crucial because it helps you maintain the kind of sustained effort that can truly transform your life over time.

Once, a devoted follower of the Buddha named Sona was practicing his religious duties with great intensity. Before becoming a monk, Sona had been a skilled sitar player, and he applied the same level of rigor and hard work to his new life as he had to mastering his musical instrument.

However, despite his hard work, Sona became frustrated because he did not feel any closer to achieving enlightenment. Realizing his disciple's struggle, the Buddha approached Sona. He asked him, "Sona, when you were a musician, what happened when the strings of your sitar were too tight?"

Sona replied, "They would snap, and the sitar would not produce any music."

"And what happened when the strings were too loose?"

"They would not produce any sound at all, and the music would not be harmonious," Sona answered.

The Buddha nodded and said, "In the same way, Sona, in your practice, if you push yourself too hard, you will break down. And if you let yourself become too lax, you will not find the path. Finding the middle way in your practice is like tuning a sitar, not too tight and not too loose."

Sona understood. He adjusted his efforts, practicing with mindfulness to not strain himself overly nor slack off, eventually finding his balance and progressing towards enlightenment.

When I first decided to start my own website, I was brimming with enthusiasm and bursting with ideas. It felt *right* – a definite calling – and I plunged into it headlong. However, I quickly realized that enthusiasm alone wasn't enough to tackle the steep learning curve and technical demands of maintaining a website. My initial burst of motivation dwindled as I faced an obstacle after another, from coding errors to content droughts. This was a classic case of misdirected effort – too much fire at the start, without a sustainable plan or the right pacing.

I was behaving like Sona, working hard and going at it with all my might. Because as shaky and uncertain as I felt in life, I was sure of one thing – hard work is necessary for living a life of purpose. And I wasn't afraid of it. I mean, I'd worked for three years at a literally backbreaking job; hard work is no stranger to me.

Fortunately, all I needed to do to get back on track was to remember that there's a blueprint for getting just the right effort.

The Four Aspects of Right Effort

A good day's work doesn't happen by accident; it happens when you really apply yourself and face life head-on. In Buddhism, right effort comes about when you leave behind the mistakes of the past, avoid it in the present, work for good, and help strengthen and reinforce good habits and deeds you've already done. It's structured around four primary tasks:

1. Preventing Negative States

Think of this first part like setting up your game plan to dodge potential pitfalls. For example, say you're starting a new diet. Before you even begin, you know late-night snacking is your weak spot. So, you stock up on healthy snacks, or maybe you decide to brush your teeth early to curb those cravings. It's all about foreseeing the hurdles and laying down strategies to leap over them smoothly.

2. Abandoning Negative States

Now, let's say you've slipped up – maybe you've binged on a whole bag of chips. It happens! This step is about catching yourself, not beating yourself up, and steering back on track. It's like realizing you've taken a wrong turn on a road trip. You don't just keep driving the wrong way; you find the next exit and correct your course. The key is to recognize the slip, learn from it, and pivot quickly without dwelling on the mistake.

3. Cultivating Positive States

Here's where you start building up the good stuff. Say you want to get better at basketball. You'd start incorporating specific drills into your practice sessions, or maybe you'd watch tutorials from pros and apply what you learn. It's about intentionally adding practices to your routine that foster growth, improvement, and ultimately, mastery. It's not enough to just stop doing what doesn't work – you've got to start doing more of what does.

4. Maintaining Positive States

This last task is about keeping up the good work. You've got a good thing going – now how do you keep it rolling? Maybe you've gotten into a great morning routine that really sets a positive tone for your day. The challenge now is to stick with it, even when you hit a day (or a week) when you just aren't feeling it. It's about making those good new habits a consistent part of your life, refining and adjusting as you go to keep it fresh and effective.

Each of these steps is about being mindful and intentional with your actions. Whether you're coding a website, writing a novel, or working towards a 5K run, applying Right Effort means you're always thinking a couple of steps ahead. You're proactive, not just reactive. You're focused on setting yourself up for success and keeping the momentum, not just dabbling around and hoping things turn out okay.

And when you really get into this groove, it's amazing how much more you can achieve and how much more enjoyable the process becomes. It's not just about the end goal – it's about making the journey there as smooth and fulfilling as possible.

EXERCISE TEN
Mindful Action Week

For one week, you're going to try a few simple, daily tweaks. Nothing fancy, just some good old mindfulness in action.

Day 1: Chill Morning Vibes

Kick off your day with something chill that's just for you. Maybe enjoy your coffee in silence instead of gulping it down, or stretch a bit. Whatever you pick, no rushing allowed.

Day 2: Block Party

Today's game is all about blocking time. Break your day into chunks and assign activities to each. Stick to one task per block—no juggling. This is about giving each thing your full attention.

Day 3: Real Talks

Chat day! Whether it's a call, a meeting, or just shooting the breeze, really listen and choose your words thoughtfully. Notice if it changes the vibe of your conversations.

Day 4: One at a Time

Do one thing at a time, all day. No multitasking. Whether it's emails, cooking, or checking texts, just focus on one task. It's surprisingly relaxing.

Day 5: Easy Does It

Time to wind down. Do something today that just makes you feel good and relaxed. Read, yoga, walk—your call. Just fully dive into relaxing mode.

Day 6: Zen Out

Give yourself a half-hour of just being. No screens, no chores, just chill and let your mind wander or not. It's all about giving yourself a break from the constant buzz.

Day 7: Pat on the Back

End the week with a treat for yourself because, hey, you've earned it. Maybe it's a tasty snack, an episode of that series you love, or a nap. Enjoy something that celebrates the work you've put in.

This little week-long adventure is all about making mindfulness fun and doable. By focusing on one thing at a time and tuning into the present moment, you're practicing Right Effort without even making a big deal out of it. By the end of the week, you might just notice you're feeling a bit sharper and a lot more zen.

What's the Point?

Each day has its own little focus to help you see how versatile Right Effort can be. From handling your morning routine without rushing to engaging deeply in conversations, you are practicing applying just the right amount of energy and attention. It's about making everything you do more intentional, which is pretty much the heart of Right Effort.

When you apply Right Effort like you do in this exercise, you start to see changes—not just in how you tackle tasks but in how you feel. Less frazzled, more in control, and maybe even a little proud of handling your biz like a mindfulness ninja. This isn't just good for your mental space; it's good for your soul, your work, your relationships...pretty much everything!

CHAPTER ELEVEN

Being Awake (Samma sati | Right Mindfulness)

"How does one stay mindful?

Where feelings are known as they arise, known as they persist, known as they pass away.

Thoughts are known as they arise, known as they persist, known as they pass away.

Perceptions are known as they arise, known as they persist, known as they pass away.

This is how a monk stays awake."

Siddharta Gautama Buddha

Let me ask you a few questions:

- How often are you fully present in your daily activities?
- What distractions usually pull you away from the present moment?
- How does being present (or not) affect your stress levels and overall well-being?
- In what areas of your life would you like to experience more clarity and focus?

If you're like most people, these questions might trigger a realization about just how often our minds wander away from the here and now. We live in a world that's buzzing with distractions – beeps from our phones, endless to-do lists, and worries that tug our attention away from the moment in front of us. It's no wonder that feeling scattered or stressed can sometimes seem like our default state.

But when you follow Buddhist principles, you can change that default. Mainly because of this aspect of the Eightfold Path: Right Mindfulness, or *Samma sati*.

Mindfulness has become a bit of a trend in recent years. Celebrities, athletes, and CEOs alike endorse "mindfulness training." Doctors and therapists integrate mindfulness into treatment plans. And countless apps such as Insight Timer, Headspace, and Calm have emerged to fill the demand for instruction in mindfulness meditation.

But mindfulness is nothing new. In fact, it's one of the core teachings of Buddhism, and one of the key ingredients of the Eightfold Path developed by the Buddha 2600 years ago.

Notice, Observe, Accept

A Buddhist Koan:

Once upon a time, as a man was walking through a forest, he saw a tiger peering out at him from the underbrush.

As the man turned to run, he heard the tiger spring after him to give chase. Barely ahead of the tiger, running for his life, our hero came to the edge of a steep cliff.

Clinging onto a strong vine, the man climbed over the cliff edge just as the tiger was about to pounce. As he was hanging over the side of the cliff, with the hungry tiger pacing above him, the man looked down and was dismayed to see another tiger, stalking the ravine far below.

Just then, a tiny mouse darted out from a crack in the cliff face above him and began to gnaw at the vine.

At that precise moment, the man noticed a patch of wild strawberries growing from a clump of earth near where he dangled. Reaching out, he plucked one. It was plump, and perfectly ripe; warmed by the sunshine. He popped the strawberry into his mouth.

It was perfectly delicious.

You've just read a classic *koan* – a type of Zen teaching story – that's all about living in the moment. Here's this guy, literally hanging between life and death, and what does he do? He enjoys a strawberry!

It's a great reminder to focus on the here and now, even when chaos is all around. No matter what kind of "tigers" or "mice" we're facing in our lives, there's always a "strawberry" – those small, sweet moments that deserve our attention and appreciation. This story's telling us to grab those moments, no matter what else is going on. Because sometimes, those moments are what life's all about.

In ancient texts, mindfulness is often described in terms of "guarding" or "watching over" the mind. This implies an active effort to keep the mind in a state of readiness and awareness, free from influences that might cloud judgment or lead to harmful actions. It's about being awake to life as it unfolds, rather than sleepwalking through it while lost in thought or reactivity.

I'll make it as simple as it could possibly be – mindfulness just means *paying attention*.

Here you are, reading a book on Buddhism. But if you pay attention, you'll notice that's not the only thing that's going on. You can feel the weight of the book or your e-reader in your hands, or on your lap. You can feel the breath going in and out of your lungs, your chest slowly rising and falling as you exchange gases with the rest of the universe. You can feel the tiny weight of the clothes you are wearing, the way your socks hold your ankles, the way your top hangs from your shoulders.

You can feel the air temperature of the room you're in. Or, if you're reading this outdoors, you can feel the warmth of the sun, the chill of the wind, the movement of the air around you. Maybe you can hear traffic outside, or the ticking of a clock. Maybe you can hear other people living their lives around you, your family doing chores or watching TV or talking. Even in a room where it seems there isn't much going on, there's always an almost infinite amount of things to pay attention to.

Thinking back to my stint at the Melbourne warehouse, I can see a glaring difference between my pre- and post-mindfulness days. When I wasn't paying attention, I truly didn't care very much about why I was shifting boxes, or where the boxes were going. I just did it for the pay. Not only that, but every hour I was there, I was wishing I was somewhere else.

But when I started practicing mindfulness and meditation, I found my attitude to the dull and repetitive work I was doing changing. I mean, let's be honest – shifting boxes around doesn't require a lot of thought, especially when you've been doing it for a while. And so my work offered another opportunity for a different kind of meditation. I started paying attention to my experiences in the moment.

The rattle of the door of a truck rolling up, and the stuffy air inside the container that smelled of plastic wrap and the wood from the pallets swirling around me. The resistance and sudden release of a plastic strap cut by my knife. The weight of a box on the dolly as I leaned it back toward my chest, and, yes, the pain in my back too as I shifted my feet…

I know it sounds strange. It sounded strange to me when I first started trying it, as if it was a trick I was playing on myself. And in a way, I guess that's what it feels like in the beginning – a mind trick. Once I saw for myself what a difference a change in mindset can make, I knew straightaway I was on the right path.

But the whole process isn't mysterious at all. It's just a matter of letting go of our judgment of things as either 'good' or 'bad' and relaxing into the serenity of the moment. You simply notice, observe, and accept.

In Part Three of this book, I'll delve deeper into mindfulness and share some practical ways to incorporate it into your life. For now, I'll leave you with this:

All of the sensations we feel are interesting, even the unpleasant ones. And while our minds race from one thing to another, dreaming of escape, wishing to be anywhere but where we are now, the whole world goes on around us. And if we're not careful, we can miss it all.

Mindfulness is how we prevent our entire lives passing us by. Using mindfulness in my own life ended up being the first step to creating a better life for myself. As Sri Lankan monk Bhante Gunarantana wisely said, "Mindfulness gives you time. Time gives you choices. Choices, skillfully made, lead to freedom."

EXERCISE ELEVEN
Mind Your Business

- Sit down in comfortable clothing.
- Sit away from loud noises and commotions — if you can.
- Put a timer on your phone. Start with five minutes and increase it by five minutes each week. Short and simple!
- Close your eyes and simply pay attention to the sensations of your body: the breeze on your skin, heat on your toes, aches in your hands or back, and so on.
- Pay attention to your natural breath as it goes in and out.
- Observe your mind and its various paths. What thoughts pop up? Look at them like fish jumping in and out of a pond.
- If you're in a loud place, simply hear the sounds without reacting to them.
- Focus on noticing the thoughts but not following them where they lead. They're just thoughts. They don't necessarily matter at all.
- Open your eyes and stretch when the alarm goes off.

What's the Point?

How often are we really in the moment? Most of the time, our minds are racing through to-do lists, replaying some awkward conversation, or worrying about stuff that hasn't even happened.

Right Mindfulness is about cutting through that noise and being fully present. It's like turning up the volume on the here and now, so you can actually experience life as it's happening.

This little sit-down you just had is the training ground. It's where you learn to notice your breath, the sensations in your body, and all the mental chatter without getting swept away by any of it. The more you practice this, the better you get at not reacting impulsively to whatever life throws at you.

This is how you start to develop a superpower called equanimity – staying cool, calm, and collected no matter what. By practicing to stay grounded in the present, even for just a few minutes each day, you're setting yourself up to handle daily life with more grace.

CHAPTER TWELVE

A Higher State of Being (Samma samadhi | Right Concentration)

"All that we are is the result of what we have thought; what we think we become."

Gautama Buddha

A s we come to the last practice in the Eightfold Path, you've hopefully seen how connected all the practices are. Each step, from Right Understanding to Right Mindfulness, all work together to guide us toward a more enlightened, peaceful way of living.

Now, we finally arrive at Right Concentration, the peak of these practices, where all the paths converge to deepen our meditation and enhance our awareness.

The term "concentration" in English comes from the Pali word "*samadhi*," which is rooted in the words "*sam-a-dha*," meaning "to bring together." And that's exactly what the practice of Right Concentration does in Buddhism. It sharpens our mental focus to a fine point, helping all the lessons from the whole path click into place. This deep focus is crucial not only for nailing those deep states of meditation but also for bringing the calm and wisdom of Buddhism into the hectic swirl of daily life.

Samadhi is a rather unique state of consciousness. SotoZen teacher John Daido Loori describes it as "a slowing down of our mental activity through single-pointed concentration."

But that single point of focus can't be just any random thing you pick. It can't be things like a desire for revenge, for example. Or a delicious meal you're craving. It's a very specific kind of focus.

Bhikkhu Bodhi, in his book "The Noble Eightfold Path," points out that *samadhi* should elevate your mind to a more enlightened, aware state through some serious mental effort. After all, the whole point of Buddhist philosophy is to help us rise above the pettiness of life and reach a higher state of consciousness. To be more in tune with the true nature of our existence and the world around us.

This form of concentration, then, is about maintaining a clear and undistracted mind that can pierce through the superficial to reach profound insights.

The end result? Wisdom. Dignity. Joy. Enlightenment.

Right Concentration vs. Right Mindfulness

Now, I'm aware that Right Concentration sounds a lot like Right Mindfulness. That's understandable, as they both have to do with mental discipline. However, they have different aims and roles in daily life.

Right Mindfulness keeps you aware of a broad range of experiences without clinging to any, just a practice of observing things as they are – no filtering or reacting based on past experiences or future expectations.

Right Concentration builds on that to deepen your ability to focus without interruption and stabilize your mind. You need this to achieve states of deep meditative absorption known as *dhyānas*.

Together, they amp up your meditative practice and help you get a better grip on what's real and what's just noise. They can help you get to a calm, collected state not just while you're meditating, but also while you're going about everything else in life.

The Four Dhyānas

So, what exactly are we aiming for when we cultivate Right Concentration? Well, the goal is to go through the four *dhyānas,* or meditative absorptions. These are like levels in a game, each one taking you deeper into meditation and closer to an incredibly calm and focused state of mind.

Think of each *dhyana* as a step up in your meditation skills – the higher you go, the more peace and clarity you get. Whether you're new to meditation or looking to deepen your practice, understanding these stages can really help you set clear goals and see some amazing changes in your mindset.

If you're a beginner, you're likely going to find it hard to focus on a single point at first – your monkey mind will probably try and distract you in many ways! So, it's a good idea to have an object to anchor your mind on, like your breath or a mantra you repeat over and over.

Some Buddhists like using *kasina*, which involves concentrating on a specific physical object or a visualized image. Common *kasinas* include discs of color, like a blue or yellow circle, or elements like fire or water. You stare at the object until the image is imprinted in your mind, and then you close your eyes and continue focusing on the visualized image.

At this initial stage, your goal is to let go of ordinary sensory awareness and rambling thoughts. I'll go deeper into the whole process of meditation later in this book, but I'll tell you right now that the point is to separate yourself from five obstacles to inner peace:

- Sensual desire
- Ill will
- Laziness
- Restlessness and worry
- Doubt

This is just like any other skill in life – the more you practice, the better you get at it. You'll find yourself able to corral your mind more quickly when it wanders and you can stay focused longer and longer.

But take note – it isn't a linear process. Some days, getting into the groove will be super easy and some days, it can feel like a real uphill battle. This was one of my mistakes early on, thinking that once I got it right, I will always get it right. But no, there were days when my focus would easily splinter at the slightest disturbance. Even when I'd already achieved perfect focus just the day before. And then I'd get so frustrated with myself!

So don't make that mistake. Allow yourself the grace to not be perfect and just trust the process. Over time, with consistent practice, your concentration will get deeper and more easily sustained.

And that's when you'll really begin to feel the difference. Once you can hold onto a meditation object without getting distracted, that's when the happiness and what they call 'rapture' kick in. It's kind of like the natural high you get when you're really nailing something. Eventually, you reach what's called *one-pointedness*, where your mind is totally dialed in on what you're meditating on, and everything else just fades away.

When you hit this level of one-pointedness, your mind then really starts to chill out. Its usual buzzing slows way down. With fewer mental distractions, you get to experience your consciousness in its pure state, just doing its thing without any interruptions. This deep focus lets you dive into even deeper states of consciousness (the *dhyanas*).

In the first couple of *dhyanas*, your pinpoint focus comes with a feeling of joy and contentment. The main difference between these stages is just how fine-tuned your concentration is.

Moving into the third *dhyana*, you keep that sharp focus and the good vibes, but you also gain a clear understanding and a balanced, even-keeled view of things – you see stuff as it really is, no spin. No personal biases. No emotional reactions. Free of social conditioning.

By the fourth *dhyana*, it's all about pure focus – your consciousness is clean and clear, unburdened by any emotional clutter.

Now, how is this whole "elevated consciousness" relevant to daily life, you might ask?

I'd say – a *lot*. For me, developing Right Concentration isn't just about the quiet moments on the mat; it's about how those skills play out in the real world. The cool calm and laser focus you get from those deeper meditation stages can seriously shape how you handle stress, make decisions, and deal with people day to day.

For instance, when you're used to holding your concentration and staying balanced like in the third and fourth *dhyanas*, big surprises or tough times don't throw you off as easily. Say something goes sideways at work or there's a bump in your personal life – instead of flipping out, you're more likely to stay chill, think things through clearly, and handle it in a way that actually fixes things instead of just freaking out.

Plus, this kind of deep focus and calm makes you way better at connecting with others. When you're not tangled up in your biases and you're not riding your emotional highs and lows, you end up being a better listener. You're really there in the conversation, not just nodding along while your mind wanders or you're silently judging.

In today's world, where everything feels urgent and emotions can run high really quick, being able to step back and see things clearly is so valuable. It's like having a secret superpower that lets you handle life's chaos with a bit more grace and smarts.

Right Concentration is at the heart of this. It's about more than just improving your meditation practice; it's about upgrading your entire approach to life. It naturally trains you to live more fully, with intention and clarity, every single day.

EXERCISE TWELVE
Candle Flame Focus

- Find a quiet room where you can sit undisturbed for at least 10-15 minutes.

- Place a candle on a stable surface at eye level in front of where you will be sitting. Ensure the room is dimly lit so that the candle flame is clearly visible.

- Sit in a comfortable position, either on a chair with your feet flat on the ground or on a cushion in a cross-legged position.

- Take a few deep breaths to relax your body and mind. Let go of any external worries or thoughts about your day.

- Light the candle and gently focus your gaze on the flame.

- Try to keep your eyes softly fixed on the flame, avoiding blinking excessively or shifting your gaze.

- Observe the characteristics of the flame – its color, shape, and movements. Notice how it flickers, how it responds to the air around it.

- Each time you find your mind wandering, gently acknowledge this without judgment and bring your focus back to the flame.

- As you become more absorbed in watching the flame, let other thoughts fade away. Continue to bring your focus back to the flame whenever distractions arise.

- With each minute, allow yourself to sink deeper into the experience, letting the flame fill your field of vision and mind.

- After 10-15 minutes, or as long as you feel comfortable, slowly shift your focus away from the candle. Take a moment to observe the room around you and gradually stand up.

- Blow out the candle safely.

- After completing this exercise, spend a few minutes reflecting on the experience. Consider how it felt to focus deeply on one point and how your mind dealt with distractions. This reflection can help you understand your current state of concentration and what you might need to work on to deepen it further.

What's the Point?

Focusing on something as simple as a candle flame trains you to tune out the noise and zero in on what truly matters at the moment. It's about creating a mental space where you can hold your attention steady, even when distractions are trying to pull you away. Think about how handy that could be during a hectic day at work or when you're trying to listen to a friend in a noisy cafe.

Practicing this kind of focused attention can help sharpen your mind for all sorts of tasks, from tackling complex projects without losing your cool to enjoying quiet moments without that nagging urge to check your phone every five seconds. It helps cultivate a sense of inner peace and control, so you're not at the mercy of a chaotic environment or a wandering mind.

PART THREE

Using Buddhism for a Better Life

*

CHAPTER THIRTEEN

*How Buddhism Improves
Your Relationships*

"Buddhism, with its non-theistic framework, grounds its ethics, not on the notion of obedience, but on that of harmony."

Bhikkhu Bodhi, The Noble Eightfold Path:
Way to the End of Suffering

I've always credited Buddhism for leading me to the most important relationship in my life – the one I have with my wife Jess. Looking back, I can see how it was kind of a domino effect.

After a few years of building up my site and Asia-hopping, I was really finding my groove in work and feeling relaxed about the future in other ways. As part of building Right Effort, I was taking better care of myself, going for a daily 10k run through the busy streets of Saigon.

It was on one of these runs that I met Jess. Stopping to tie my shoes one day by the canal, I tripped on the hem of the skirt of a young lady walking to work. I apologized profusely, and she smiled at me, waving away my apology. I could've left it at that, but there was something about her that kept me rooted to the spot. And in just those few minutes, we started talking.

We agreed to meet up again a few days after that at a nice restaurant in the Phú Nhuận neighborhood. And it was there that I had a really pleasant discovery – Jess told me she loved Hack Spirit and had been reading it for months. She was over the moon to meet the man behind the blog, and it was amazing to connect over something we both found important.

I sat looking at this entrancing woman and feeling like I was right where I needed to be in life. She was the complete opposite of me, and way more understanding and funny.

Anyway, long story short – our dates got longer, more intimate, and we began discussing a serious relationship. It all happened naturally and felt so right.

Jess and I were married last year and we couldn't be happier. We're taking life as it comes and finding our bond grows stronger by the day.

See how it all came together? If I hadn't followed the Buddha's Eightfold Path, maybe I never would have met her. Right Speech and Right Livelihood led me to start my website. Right Effort guided me to take care of my physical health, which is why I was running that day. Right Mindfulness helped me to appreciate this beautiful woman from the moment we started talking.

So I can honestly say that if it wasn't for Buddhism, I wouldn't have the marriage I have today. Of course, our marriage isn't perfect – whose is? But we're both committed and we apply what we've learned from Buddhist teachings to be better partners to each other.

So, how can Buddhism improve your relationships?

For starters, meditation quiets the constant mental chatter that we all carry around with us. It silences the voice that says, *She always does this,* or *He did that on purpose to provoke me.*

When we're not overwhelmed by negative emotions, it's easier to hear what our friend or partner is really saying. The more centered and peaceful we are, the easier it becomes to avoid drama and practice lovingkindness to the people around us.

Let's take a look at the other ways Buddhist principles can enhance your personal relationships.

Compassion

Most of the world's biggest religions emphasize the importance of acting with compassion and treating people around you with respect and kindness. Buddhism is no different. While it can often seem like Buddhism is all about focusing on yourself, it also contains an ethical component that guides its followers on how to live in harmony with the world around them.

The fundamental Buddhist principles we've discussed earlier in this book are key to treating anyone with respect. But they are especially important in the relationships we have with those closest to us. And compassion is a big part of that.

Compassion towards your loved ones starts by re-framing the situation.

Let's take for example, a friend who's late for your coffee date. Instead of grumbling, "She's always late!" or "She should've left earlier," try thinking,

"Man, traffic must be crazy," or "She's got a lot on her plate."

There's a lot of research showing we're often kinder to ourselves than to others. We've always got a great excuse for why we're late, right? But when someone else is late, it's easier to get annoyed. It's easier to focus on the hurt we feel instead of what might be going on with them. I know myself that when I start to get frustrated with something my wife has done or hasn't done, thinking about it from her point of view usually makes that frustration go away.

One of the most reliable predictors of how long a relationship will last is the attitude people take into it. In successful marriages, both partners develop the habit of searching for what their spouse is doing right and what they can be grateful for, instead of looking for mistakes or reasons to criticize. Practice compassion towards the people around you as often as possible and you will find your relationships flow much better.

Lovingkindness

The Story of the Quarreling Monks

Once, during the time of the Buddha, there was a group of monks who lived together in a monastery. These monks began to quarrel over various small issues. Their disagreements escalated, leading to harsh words and disturbed peace within the community. The atmosphere became so toxic that it not only affected the monks but also the lay people who visited.

The Buddha, upon learning about this discord, decided to intervene directly to restore harmony. He approached the quarreling monks and shared a parable about the dangers of anger and the importance of harmony and loving-kindness.

He told them of a past life story where he was a king who faced an invasion. When advised by his ministers to attack the invaders, he instead chose to spread messages of peace and sent gifts to the invading king. Moved by this gesture of kindness, the invading king halted his attack and peace was restored. The Buddha explained that like the king, the monks had the choice to respond to disagreements with anger or with loving-kindness.

He then taught them the practice of Metta meditation, instructing them to cultivate thoughts of loving-kindness towards themselves and each other. The Buddha emphasized that Metta was like a soothing balm that could heal the wounds of the heart and restore peace. He guided them to extend feelings of kindness beyond their circle, to their friends, to neutral persons, and even to their enemies.

Taking the Buddha's teachings to heart, the monks began to practice Metta meditation earnestly. Over time, the atmosphere of the monastery transformed. The monks began to speak kindly to each other, their *minds softened, and the peace in the community was restored.*

The principle of lovingkindness, or "*Metta*" in Pali, is a fundamental aspect of Buddhist philosophy. It represents a form of unconditional love and friendliness toward all beings, free from self-interest. Lovingkindness is not just a feeling but a way of being and relating to the world, which Buddhists believe can profoundly transform individual lives and the larger community.

Metta begins with cultivating a kind and loving attitude towards oneself and gradually extends this benevolence outward to friends, acquaintances, strangers, and even those with whom we may have conflicts. The ultimate goal is to develop an attitude of lovingkindness that pervades our thoughts, actions, and speech consistently.

You would think that cultivating lovingkindness can only benefit the person receiving it, right? But the added beauty of it is that you also benefit! That's because it purifies your mind and helps dissolve the nasty feelings of anger, resentment, and dissatisfaction. The more *metta* grows in you, the smaller and smaller the barriers between you and other people get; you'll feel a sense of interconnectedness and peace.

In one word – harmony.

In practice, *Metta* is often cultivated through meditation. A common method involves focusing on phrases that express goodwill, such as:

- "May I be happy"
- "May I be safe"
- "May all beings be happy"

The meditation itself is simply about noticing yourself and others, accepting them as they are, loving them, and wishing good things for them. Don't feel like you have to do or try to do anything. Just exist with a mindset of love and friendliness.

You will begin by feeling love and kindness for yourself, then direct these feelings outward – to family, to friends, to colleagues and acquaintances, to strangers, and even to your enemies.

If it helps, you can imagine it like a radial ocean wave that ripples outwards in wider and wider circles. That wave has a center point – YOU, the source of these good thoughts and well wishes. And with each ripple, your sentiments wash over more and more people out there.

"May you be happy." "May you be safe." "May all beings be happy." These thoughts are so powerful that they can break down the walls we've built around us because of ego- and aversion-related issues.

Once the meditation ends and you return to your daily activities, you may very well feel moved to apply these feelings of lovingkindness in your actions.

Whenever I finish a lovingkindness meditation, I usually find myself really motivated to act on those feelings. It's like I want to keep that calm and warmth going, whether I'm at work or just hanging out at home. I make a conscious effort to be more patient, to listen better, and to give people the benefit of the doubt. It's amazing how these small changes can really lift my spirits and improve my interactions throughout the day.

You can also be a little more active in your approach to developing loving kindness. One great way to do this is with a lovingkindness walk. Just choose a route where you feel safe and comfortable for your walk and then set an intention before you begin walking, such as: "*I will use this walk to spread lovingkindness to myself and others.*"

The process is basically the same as a sitting lovingkindness meditation, except that you get the added bonus of silently repeating the phrases to the strangers you encounter as you pass them by. And maybe even share a smile or two!

You can do this in as little as 15 minutes, so it's something you can do first thing in the morning, during your lunch break, or at the end of the day.

What I love about this exercise is that it forces you to interact with the world as it is. It's easy to be loving and kind in the comfort of your own house, but it's in the chaos of the world and in interactions with other people that this practice becomes truly meaningful.

Dealing with Enemies

"May my enemies be well, happy, and peaceful. May no harm come to them. May no difficulties come to them. May no problems come to them. May they always meet with success. May they also have patience, courage, understanding, and determination to meet and overcome inevitable difficulties, problems, and failures in life."

- *Bhante Henepola Gunaratana, Mindfulness in Plain English*

"You have heard that it was said, 'Eye for an eye, and tooth for a tooth.' But I tell you, do not resist an evil person. If anyone slaps you on the right cheek, turn to them the other cheek also…You have heard that it was said, 'Love your neighbor and hate your enemy.' But I tell you, love your enemies and pray for those who persecute you."

- *Matthew 5:38-39*

Religious traditions from across the world – including both Buddhism and Christianity – have developed seemingly nonsensical attitudes of compassion and forgiveness toward enemies.

Why should we love our enemies or wish that no harm may befall them? Why should we wish them success in their endeavors – when those endeavors might very well include attacking us??

From a Buddhist perspective, there are several explanations for wishing your enemies well.

First, it does you no good to hold onto anger or resentment, even if the other person deserves it. The only thing that leads to is baggage – you'll be carrying tension and unhappiness within you. So it's best to set aside grudges, if only for your own sake.

Second, you can use and appreciate the opportunities that your enemies provide for you to practice your patience and lovingkindness!

Look, there's nothing challenging or unusual about treating people you love kindly – that comes naturally. People you dislike, however…now that's a real challenge. It gives you the chance to deepen your practice.

Third, ask yourself why you consider certain people your enemies. Are they rude, short-tempered, selfish, or boastful? Likely, these unpleasant characteristics stem from various problems in their own lives. Perhaps they're rude and impatient because they hate their job. Perhaps they're boastful because they're deeply insecure about themselves.

In any case, by wishing that your enemies be "well, happy, and peaceful," by wishing that they encounter no difficulties or problems, you're effectively wishing to remove the conditions that made them your enemies in the first place. Makes total sense, doesn't it?

"Practically speaking, if all of your enemies were well, happy, and peaceful, they would not be your enemies. If they were free from problems, pain, suffering, affliction, neurosis, psychosis, paranoia, fear, tension, anxiety, etc., they would not be your enemies. The practical approach toward your enemies is to help them overcome their problems, so you can live in peace and happiness."

- *Bhante Henepola Gunaratama, Mindfulness in Plain English*

Fourth, remind yourself that you see hostile people and situations only from your perspective and do not know the whole story.

Are you open to the possibility that you could have misunderstood something or misjudged someone else's actions? Have you taken some perceived slight too personally? And even if you are convinced of your own righteousness, are you at least open to the idea that returning hatred with hatred does nothing to improve the situation?

Finally, keep in mind that if you decide to struggle against your enemies, your struggles will be endless.

As Nagarjuna said, "Although you may spend your life killing, you will not exhaust all your foes." I don't know about you, but the idea of struggling forever with anger and heaviness in my heart doesn't sound appealing.

Focus and attention

If you've been following a daily meditation practice, you should find that you're gradually becoming able to focus for longer on one thing. It becomes easier to direct your attention where you want it to go, instead of jumping about everywhere. Now, we're going to apply that focus to your relationships.

In any relationship, each person is constantly bidding for the other's time and attention. When your mother calls to tell you the neighborhood gossip, your friend wants to show you their vacation snaps, or your partner comes home and complains about their day, they're asking for your attention.

In the course of busy modern life, we often only give our loved ones half our attention. We respond to statements with *Uh-huh* and *Sure,* we don't ask questions or show interest, we keep doing other things at the same time.

When you only give your friends and family some of your attention, you're sending them a message that they're not your highest priority. Relationships have to be nurtured, and that means spending time and energy on them.

Start by spending ten minutes every day giving your partner or family your full attention. Put down your phone, stop whatever you're doing, and just listen to them. If you eat dinner together then that's a good daily opportunity, but any time will do. Show an interest in the things that are important to them. Ask questions. Let them feel validated. Make your relationships a priority, and watch them blossom.

As I mentioned earlier, I owe the most important relationship in my life to Buddhism. But the teachings of this ancient tradition can help you strengthen and deepen any relationship you have, whether it's with a romantic partner, your parents, your children, or even your enemies. If you follow the ethical teachings of Buddhism correctly, your relationships with other people will naturally improve.

CHAPTER FOURTEEN

*How Mindfulness Can
Change Your Life*

"*Zen pretty much comes down to three things - everything changes; everything is connected; pay attention.*"

Jane Hirshfield

I 've already touched on mindfulness earlier in this book, but let's dig a little deeper into it, as it's such a central practice in the Buddhist way of life.

Our minds wander constantly.

As you go for a hike, your mind might be replaying memories: a recent argument with your partner, a vacation you took last month, a worrying conversation with a friend.

As you sit at your desk at work, maybe you're daydreaming about winning the lottery or planning ahead to what you'll eat for dinner.

As you drive home, your mind might remain in the office, still brainstorming solutions and composing emails.

How often do you truly live in the moment with complete focus on what you are doing? Eight hours per day? Three Hours? One?

For most people, that number is quite small.

Harvard researcher Matt Killingsworth developed an app called Track Your Happiness to get some data on what makes us happy. At random intervals over the course of the day, the app prompted its 15,000 users to indicate what they were doing, whether their minds were wandering, and how happy they were.

The results indicate that mind wandering is very common: Approximately 47% of the time, people are focused on something other than what they are actually doing.

Plus, Killingsworth noticed a striking link between happiness and mindfulness. People who were mindful, who were concentrating on what they were doing, reported higher levels of happiness.[1]

This study is only one of many confirming what Buddhists already know: that mindfulness is a key component of living your best, happiest, most fulfilled life. To be mindful means to give your mind a break from rehashing the past or worrying about the future. Instead, we appreciate and accept the present. To be mindful means to realize that our lives consist of moments, and that each present moment is all we have. If we sleepwalk through our lives, going through our days on autopilot, we will inevitably miss an awful lot.

The truth is, we think that our lives are made up of big events, achievements, and exciting experiences. But they aren't.

That's part of being alive, sure. But most of it is far smaller and much less grand. This is your real life, right here and right now. Whatever you're doing in the moment is the only reality you have.

The Zen Buddhist teacher Alan Watts wrote:

"The future is a concept, it doesn't exist. There is no such thing as tomorrow. There never will be, because time is always now. That's one of the things we

discover when we stop talking to ourselves and stop thinking. We find there is only present, only an eternal now."

That's a profound realization that comes directly from Buddhist mindfulness practices.

Let's do a thought exercise.

When was the last time you thought about the future?

I don't mean anything big, necessarily. It could be something simple, like thinking about what you're going to have for dinner tonight, or what you'll do on the weekend. Alternatively, it can be something bigger, like where you want to live, the kind of person you want to marry, or what you want to do for a living. If you're anything like me, you'll realize that you spend a huge amount of your time thinking about the future, whether the short-term or the long-term.

Before I discovered Buddhism, working in that warehouse, my thoughts were all about the future and the escape it promised from the drudgery of my job. But whether I was looking forward to a ham sandwich at lunchtime or thinking about the weekend when I could watch my team Essendon play, the future was my drug of choice. Chances are, you think of the future several times each day, in one way or another.

Now, ask yourself, how much do you think about the past?

Again, I'm not talking about the things you learned in history class. I mean your past. Something somebody said to you, last week or last year. Something from your childhood, a favorite toy or a beloved grandparent. A relationship that went bad. A vacation you wish you could relive.

In fact, you can even try this exercise to understand just how much you are thinking about the past and the future instead of the present:

- **Set Up a Tracking System**: Divide a page in your notebook into three columns labeled: "Present," "Past," and "Future". You can also create a simple table for each day if you prefer.
- **Set Reminders**: Use a timer or reminder app to alert you every hour (or at regular intervals that suit your schedule). These reminders will prompt you to pause and reflect on your thoughts.
- **Check-In with Your Thoughts**: When the reminder goes off, take a moment to pause whatever you are doing. Close your eyes if possible and take a few deep breaths to center yourself.
- **Categorize Your Thoughts**: Reflect on what you were thinking about just before the reminder. Categorize your thoughts into one of the three columns below:

- ○ Present: Thoughts focused on what you're doing or experiencing right now
- ○ Past: Thoughts about past events, memories, regrets, or reflections
- ○ Future: Thoughts about upcoming events, plans, worries, or anticipations

- **Write Down Your Thoughts**: Briefly jot down the content of your thought in the appropriate column. For example:

  - ○ Present: "Focused on typing an email."
  - ○ Past: "Thinking about a conversation I had yesterday."
  - ○ Future: "Worrying about an upcoming meeting."

- **Continue Throughout the Day**: Repeat this process every time your reminder goes off. If you catch yourself thinking about the past or future between reminders, feel free to note that down as well.

- **Review Your Entries**: At the end of the day, reflect on how much of your mental energy is spent on the past, present, and future. Notice any patterns or common themes in your thoughts.

- **Reflect on the Impact**: Consider how your tendency to think about the past or future affects your stress levels, mood, and overall well-being. Ask yourself:

- How does thinking about the past/future impact my ability to be present?
- What triggers my past- or future-oriented thoughts?
- How can I bring more of my focus to the present moment?

The point is, throughout the day, our thoughts shuttle back-and-forth between past and future. But as the Buddha realized, as Watts and other teachers have pointed out, there's really no such thing. Your memories of the past and your dreams of the future can only occur now, in the present. And the future you are working toward will never come. Because when it finally does arrive, it will be the present. And if you've never learned how to enjoy the present moment, you won't enjoy the future when it gets here, either.

Mindfulness is also closely connected to Buddhist ethics of loving kindness, compassion, and care for oneself and others. Cultivating a practice of mindfulness often goes hand in hand with developing a more generous outlook on the world.

Practices such as meditation, yoga, and chanting show us the path to obtaining a state of mindfulness. Of course, even if we do yoga, chant, and meditate every day, that doesn't mean we're going to achieve mindfulness. These practices promote the ability to be mindful, but most of us have a hard time quieting the mind. It is a practice and a discipline all on its own.

Let's break down some of the key benefits of mindfulness and how it puts you back in control of your life.

1. Reduce rumination

Ruminating is when you repetitively go over a thought or problem without finding the solution. Some might call it obsessing. When ruminating takes over (when you're not being mindful), you get stuck in a rut: you replay thoughts about that project you messed up, or all the bad luck you've had this week, or the things you're dreading.

Numerous studies have shown that mindfulness reduces rumination, which is a major contributor to stress and anxiety disorders.

Mindfulness allows you to accept the part of you that ruminates, without listening to it. Your mind may want to talk and talk ad nauseam, but you can observe these thoughts, feelings, and worries from a distance. In other words, just because you feel something doesn't mean it's real.

And it's not about fighting with yourself and your own mind. Mindfulness teaches a better way. You can accept your thoughts as they are without trying to change them, but when you do that, a magical thing happens: your thoughts lose their power over you.

2. Reduce stress

When you're more mindful, you chip away at the inner voices of your "monkey mind," the part of your brain that leaps from thought to thought just as a monkey swings from branch to branch.

There have been several dozen studies exploring mindfulness-based stress reduction. Researchers have found that mindfulness-based cognitive therapy is an effective treatment in many clinical disorders.[2]

Practicing mindfulness at home for smaller issues you face daily is great for your mental health. You may even prevent some clinical mental disorders and reduce negative emotions that decrease your quality of life.

The next time you start to feel angry, anxious, or frustrated, try exploring the feelings that come up rather than feeding them. Where does the tightness sit? In your throat or belly? Scan down your body, noticing tense muscles. Notice your breath: Is it deep and even, or shallow and ragged?

This is mindfulness. Neither avoiding these feelings, nor getting lost in them.

3. Increase focus

Cultivating a practice of mindfulness can enhance your powers of concentration in other areas of your life. Through meditation, you learn how to keep your focus on one thing at a time and not be easily distracted.

Researchers have compared a group of experienced mindfulness meditators with a control group that had no experience. The results indicated that the group of experienced meditators had a greater attention span.[3] You might find that regular mindfulness practice can sharpen your mind and make you better at paying attention to details.

When you practice mindfulness in a controlled setting, you'll begin to figure out how it works – the feeling of expansion in the mind and the relaxation of all the muscles in the body. Once you get the hang of focusing and centering in your quiet place, you can start using it where it really counts in high-stakes situations. When life becomes overwhelming and everyone is demanding something from you, you can briefly center yourself. Instead of surrendering to the "monkey mind" and panicking, you can quickly focus and manage priorities.

4. Increase emotional strength

Maybe you have extreme sensitivities or struggle to control your emotions. This makes it a challenge to flow through life without a care in the world. Extreme emotional sensitivity makes it difficult to enjoy life.

Again, this is an area in which mindfulness can help.

Researchers have connected mindfulness meditation and self-reported mindfulness to attentional functioning and emotional elasticity. They found that people who practice mindfulness have less emotional reactivity.[4]

This doesn't mean that you have less compassion; rather, you simply have more resilience and ability to cope with life's inevitable trials. You're able to help others in a crisis because you remain calm, without panicking or freezing.

Through mindfulness, you can also begin to work through repressed emotions. Instead of shying away from them, you learn to feel them and let them move through you. As you practice this more and more, you don't hit those emotional edges that trigger hurt, anger, and sadness.

I know it's not easy. We all have those parts of our lives that are difficult to face, those emotions we would rather not deal with. But mindfulness meditation can make it easier to face what bothers you most and deal with it in a healthy way.

5. The freedom to live fully

When you hide away past emotions, you essentially put yourself in a cage of your own making. The only way out is to push through the uncomfortable truths you've been repressing. If you go near the edge of the cage, you feel extreme discomfort. In that place of discomfort, you can finally deal with past trauma and pain.

Mindfulness is the key to escape from your emotional cage.

The more you deal with past emotions through mindfulness the less emotional disturbance can occur. Emotional disturbance is based on something that happened to you long ago, something you haven't let go of. Through mindfulness, you can let go and then you can be free.

6. Relationship satisfaction

You may notice that a person's ability to be mindful can be a predictor of how good a relationship will be.

When you practice mindfulness, you're more likely to respond well to any challenges or stress that arise in a relationship. You're aware of your emotions and can communicate your feelings without blame. Studies have found that mindfulness can protect you from overreacting to relationship conflicts.[5]

Let's face it, relationships aren't always easy, but when you build mindfulness into your life, you can ease conflict. Even if there's no immediate or obvious solution, you won't become anxious. You won't fall into the storytelling of your ego and cause an unnecessary fight.

What you will do is truly listen to what the person is saying without immediately lashing out in defense. Instead, you mindfully consider how you can help your partner and strengthen the relationship you've built.

If you experience strong emotions coming up, you don't immediately react. You feel these emotions out instead. You pay attention to whatever tension comes up in the body and try to understand why you're affected. This helps you to own what's yours and not react to other people's drama.

7. What you can see, you can change

When you're willing to look inside yourself, you can see what is and isn't working. When you feel insecure, instead of avoiding the feeling, you can investigate. As you practice more and more, your mind will begin to reveal where these feelings really come from. You may recall a moment in your childhood where you felt abandoned or ignored, or realize that you never learned a particular skill.

When you can grasp what's really going on and what emotions are stuck in your body, you can get rid of them for good. It only takes confronting these old bits of energy to truly be free of them forever. This is how you evolve and move forward with your life without fears that make very little sense.

You can be calm in a situation that would normally stress you out. Life is always changing, but when you're open to changing too, it's not so uncomfortable. You can quickly adjust and even benefit from it.

Change is always challenging. Sometimes, it can seem like you are irreversibly stuck with your old habits, and no matter how hard you try, you can never break free of them.

That isn't true. It may take time – years, even. But little by little, regular practice can help you not only identify thought patterns that aren't good for you, but gradually change them, too.

Simple mindfulness practices

Mindfulness is a genuinely life-changing practice. My own mindfulness journey began when I started meditating. In my little Melbourne apartment, I made a tiny space for myself to meditate each day, even if only for five minutes.

And over time, I found that meditation practice also made me more mindful throughout the day. However, you can be mindful without having to sit down and meditate.

Here I'll outline some simple yet incredibly effective mindfulness practices that you can incorporate into your daily life.

Waking Up

Do you wake up with a smile, feeling excited for the new day? Or do you roll groaning out of bed, feeling groggy and irritable?

So many of us feel incredibly cranky before our first cup or two of coffee. If you're not a morning person, you might benefit from transforming your morning routine into a more mindful one. If you start the day in a way that gives you a sense of peace and fulfillment, you take that attitude into the rest of your day too.

Here are some ideas to help you start your day off with mindfulness:

- Leave yourself plenty of time. Allow yourself to enjoy a peaceful morning instead of hitting snooze five times then rushing around.

- As you awaken, breathe in and out deeply, focusing on the sensation of the breath. Feel the weight of your body as you lie in bed, the weight of your head on your pillow. Allow yourself a few moments to just exist. Try not to think about the day ahead and everything it holds. Just focus on your breathing and exist.

- Get out of bed and perform a few gentle stretches to warm up your body – shoulder circles, arm circles, hip circles, ankle circles.

- Meditate, even if only for 5 or 10 minutes. You can fit this in while you're waiting for your eggs to cook, or leave the house a little earlier and spend a few minutes meditating in the car before your commute.

- If you walk to work or school, try a walking meditation to get you into the right headspace for the day. There's more on walking meditations in the next section.
- Reflect on your goals for the day. When you focus on the things that are important to you every morning, you make it less likely that you'll get sidetracked during the day by other tasks.
- Eat a healthy breakfast and make a cup of herbal tea. Ideally, allow yourself enough time to eat and drink mindfully instead.
- If time allows, get some exercise. The morning is a good time to go for a walk or jog or to practice yoga.

Sound like a lot? So many of us are in a hurry every morning, frantically showering and rushing off to school or work. It may require some conscious effort and lifestyle changes to slow your morning down from its hectic pace and start your day with mindfulness.

You might even be skeptical that these habits will make any difference in your life.

In that case, why not try a month-long experiment?

Consider shifting your bedtime and waking times earlier (by as little as 15 minutes per day) and gradually introduce several of the habits listed above. With some practice, you'll likely find that mindful mornings pave the way for the rest of the day.

Breathing

This one's as simple as breathing in and breathing out with a conscious awareness of your breath. We breathe all the time but usually hardly notice unless something is wrong—if we're short of breath after a steep hike, for instance, or if we have bad allergies.

First, take stock of your posture and the quality of your breath as it is now. Sit down on a chair or couch in your usual posture, and ask yourself:

Is my breath deep or shallow? Smooth and even or ragged?

Take several deep breaths. How easy is it to breathe deeply? Does this feel natural? Does the air fill my upper lungs (making the chest rise) or does it flow fully into my lungs (making the stomach rise)?

Once you've made these observations, sit up straight or stand upright, with your head aligned over your shoulders and hips. You might imagine that you're a marionette puppet, with a string running down through your head and body, pulling you up toward the ceiling.

Now continue to breathe deeply and observe your breath. With correct posture, your lungs should be free to expand fully, pushing your abdomen out as you inhale and pulling it in as you exhale.

Buddhist practice encourages awareness of our breathing. If your breathing is shallow and your posture bad, your body can start to produce a stress response.

Diaphragmatic breathing, where you breathe deeply from the bottom of your chest, reduces heart rate and anxiety and lowers blood pressure. Taking a few moments during the day to breathe and relax will make you less stressed and more able to focus on the task in front of you.

As we inhale, we are fully aware of the in-breath; as we exhale, we are fully aware of the out-breath. We feel the air as it fills our lungs, and notice the rising and falling of our torsos. The breath serves as an anchor that grounds us in the moment, in the here and now. Conscious breathing is central to Buddhist principles and the practice of meditation.

Done regularly, conscious breathing and meditation lower the risk of stress-related illnesses like depression, cardiovascular disease and strokes.

Conscious breathing may feel awkward at first, but with time and practice, this awkwardness will pass. You may find it helpful to use simple phrases to help keep your focus.

For example:

- "Rising…falling…rising…falling" – to imitate the rising and falling of your chest as you breathe.
- "Breathing in…breathing out…" or more simply, "In…out… in…out…"
- "One…two…three…four…" up to ten, and then start over. Think "one" as you inhale, "two" as you exhale, and so on.

I'll return to breathing in the next chapter on meditation.

Eating Mindfully

Have you ever looked down at an empty plate, only to wonder where your food went? You don't even remember eating it, and you definitely didn't enjoy it.

Mindful eating puts you in tune with your body so you can listen to its signals. It will help you lose weight without the constant stress of dieting, and prevent you from snacking mindlessly. Mindful eating helps people cope with eating problems like anorexia, and reduce the anxiety and guilt some of us feel around eating.

And maybe best of all, it will also help you enjoy your food more.

Taking the time, even just for a couple of seconds, to focus on the taste and texture of your food helps you appreciate it completely. When you eat mindfully, you may find yourself surprised by just how delicious some of the things you normally eat really are. And all you needed to do was focus.

Here is how to bring a mindful attitude to the next meal you eat:

- Don't eat in front of your computer. If you're concentrating on work, that's a guaranteed way not to taste what you're eating. The same goes for entertainment. Turn off the TV and eat at the table, using real flatware and china.
- Totally focus on at least the first three bites. Take a moment to savor your food – What does it taste like? Is it spicy? Sweet? Use all your senses and be attentive to the color, texture, and smell.
- If you normally shovel food into your mouth, then eat more slowly. Smaller bites help you to really taste the food. Stop every so often to take a few breaths or a sip of water.
- Try eating as though you had paid a lot of money for the food in a fancy restaurant. If this was world-class cuisine, you'd want to enjoy every bite and remember it, right? Even if you're not a great chef, the aim is still to enjoy what you're eating as much as possible.

Fair warning – mindful eating does take longer. But it leaves you feeling full and satisfied, so that you're not tempted to snack during the day or get up for something to eat because you're bored.

If you don't have much time, try to eat at least two mindful meals every week, and scale up from there.

Getting Down and Getting Up

When was the last time you sat on the floor?

We spend so much time on the floor as babies, toddlers, and small children. We crawl and play and move with ease all over the floor and ground. We use our arms to get around just as much as our legs.

As we grow up, however, most of us lose our easy familiarity with ground movement and become accustomed to sitting on chairs and couches.

"There is a particular feeling of time stopping when you get your body down on the floor...Maybe it's because being on the floor is so foreign to us that it breaks up our habitual neurological patterning and invites us to enter into this moment through a sudden opening in what we might call the body door."

- *Jon Kabat-Zinn, Wherever You Go There You Are, 157*

Try this: For thirty minutes every day, sit on the floor.

Want to watch TV? Cool, you can watch it from the floor. Need to get some work done? No problem, you can bring your laptop or books or whatever you need to the floor. Time to cook dinner? Put the chopping board on a low table and kneel on the floor while you chop vegetables.

With repeated time and practice, you'll regain your youthful ease of movement and flexibility.

You might also find that sitting on the floor encourages a heightened awareness of how you're sitting. When you're in a big comfortable desk chair or a cushioned sofa, it's all too easy to forget about your posture. You slouch, or push your head and neck forward, or develop a muscle imbalance, and the cushions all around prevent you from noticing.

In contrast, you will actually notice how you are sitting on the hard floor or ground because you are unused to it. Which positions are most comfortable? How long can you maintain any one position?

You'll probably find yourself naturally shifting positions occasionally—which is much better for your neck and back than staying cramped and static in your chair.

You can also use your time on the floor to engage in mindful stretching exercises. Gently stretch your hamstrings, hips, and other tight areas. I used to do this when I first started meditating in my Melbourne apartment, and it's a habit that helped me stay more conscious of my posture and body position to this day.

As you stretch, remain attentive to your body and breathing. Experiment with shifting positions in rhythm with your breath. How does your body feel and move?

Working Out

Paying attention can often seem like a passive thing to do, but part of the power of mindfulness is that you can bring it into almost any aspect of your life.

Even when you're at your most active, you can pay attention to what you're doing and get the benefits of mindfulness as well as the physical exercise you're performing.

In fact, being more mindful of how you use your body can motivate you to take better care of it and put you more in touch with your physical side.

Here's how you can make your workout boost your mindfulness skills:

- **Be clear about your aim**

Start your workout with a clear intention. As you prepare, consciously envision how you want to guide your session. For example, if you're about to go for a bike ride, you might set the intention to breathe deeply and notice the sensation of the breeze, the warmth of the sun, and the scenery passing by. If you're swimming, you could focus on paying attention to each stroke and the sound and feel of the water surrounding you. Setting a clear aim helps ground your activity in mindfulness from the very beginning.

- **Warm up (5 minutes)**

Begin with simple warm-up exercises like jumping jacks or stretching. Concentrate on matching the rhythm of your breath to your movement. This rhythmic alignment helps stabilize your brain activity, heart rate, and nervous system, preparing your body and mind for the workout ahead.

- **Settle into a rhythm (10 to 15 minutes)**

As you pick up the intensity of your workout, continue to coordinate your breath with your movements. If you find this challenging, focus solely on your breathing for a few minutes until you find your rhythm. This harmony between breath and movement is crucial for maintaining mindfulness throughout your exercise.

- **Challenge yourself (10 to 15 minutes)**

Push yourself by increasing speed, doing more repetitions, or lifting heavier weights, depending on your activity. Pay attention to how alert and alive you feel when you challenge your limits. This phase is about embracing the effort and being fully present in the sensations of exertion.

- **Cool down (5 minutes)**

Gradually slow down your pace until you come to a

standstill. Use this time to notice how your body feels and to drink in your surroundings. Cooling down mindfully helps transition your body from the heightened state of exercise back to a resting state.

- **Rest (5 minutes)**

Take a moment to rest and quietly recognize the symphony of sensations flowing in and around you. Practice naming what you feel and sense. This final step is about appreciating the state of wakefulness and aliveness that comes from mindful exercise.

Driving

For many of us, driving is a major source of daily stress. In fact, driving can seem like one of the least Buddhist activities you'll ever do. After all, driving is all about getting somewhere else. Rushing to work or hurrying to an appointment are almost the opposite of being mindful and present.

But that's exactly why bringing mindfulness into your driving can be so powerful. By staying in the present moment, even if you're running late, you can control your emotions and your reactions to the other drivers on the road. Not only does this help develop your mindfulness practice, but it will also keep you safer.

Sounds simple, right? But, as any harried driver knows, it's easier said than done. When you're right in the thick of traffic trying to get somewhere on time, it's all too easy to get caught up in anxiety and frustration. Or maybe even rage, if someone rudely cuts you off.

So let's break it down into simple steps that are easy to remember:

- **Take a deep breath**

This simple action brings more oxygen into your body and creates a space between the traffic-induced stress and your reaction to it. In this space lies the potential for perspective and choice.

- **Ask yourself what you need**

In that moment of stress, ask yourself what you need. It could be a sense of safety, ease, or relief. Identifying your need helps bring balance to your state of mind.

- **Give yourself what you need**

Once you've identified what you need, take steps to provide it for yourself. If you need ease, scan your body for any tension and soften it. Adjust your body as needed to feel more comfortable. Sprinkle in some phrases of self-compassion, such as, "*May I be at ease, may I be safe, may I feel happy.*" This can help reduce tension and promote a sense of well-being.

- **Recognize the humanity of other drivers**

Look around and recognize that all the other drivers are just like you. Everyone wants to feel safe, at ease, and to be happy. You might see drivers who look agitated, but you might also see someone singing or smiling, which can help dissipate your own stress. Extend the same compassion you offered yourself to others, silently saying, "*May you be at ease, may you feel safe, may you be happy.*"

- **Take another deep breath**

Finally, take another deep breath. In just 15 seconds, these simple tips can help turn your mood around. When you feel the frustration of traffic rising, choose what you need to work on and offer that condition to others. Breathe in, breathe out, and you've sown a seed of happiness.

Hopefully, you can see how mindfulness isn't some vague wishy-washy spiritual practice, but can instead be a part of your daily life. In fact, that's how it works best. By incorporating mindfulness into your everyday activities, no matter how mundane, you will gradually reprogram your brain to focus on the present. And when you do that, you open yourself up to living a better, more fulfilling, more joyful life.

The Buddhist practice of mindfulness is one of the key insights of this Eastern philosophy, and it is closely linked to another famous Buddhist practice - that of meditation. In the next chapter, we'll look at how meditation not only makes it easier to be mindful, but can also guide you to become a better version of yourself.

CHAPTER FIFTEEN

The Power of Meditation

"Meditation brings wisdom; lack of meditation leaves ignorance. Know well what leads you forward and what holds you back, and choose the path that leads to wisdom."

Siddharta Gautama Buddha

It's quiet.

You're sitting upright on the floor, holding your back straight, your eyes closed, trying to keep your legs crossed in that lotus position that Buddhist monks make look so effortless.

You can feel some strain in your hips and knees, but you try to shut it out. You try to shut everything out.

Maybe you have some music playing, some soft ambient tune that YouTube promised would help you meditate. Maybe you're burning some incense, letting the strong but pleasant smell fill your nostrils.

You breathe. That's easy enough.

You breathe again.

In. Out. In. Out.

That's what you're supposed to do, right?

Wow. This is… kind of boring, isn't it?

What was it the book said? Are you supposed to chant or something? Mantas - isn't that what they call them? No, *mantras*. Mantas are those huge rays that live in the sea.

Wouldn't it be great to see the Great Barrier Reef someday? Do they have sharks there? Paula just went diving with her husband in Mexico, but you're not sure you would ever have the guts to go underwater like that.

Paula was off sick last week, and you tried to cover for her, but it's not going to be easy to finalize the project in time for this week's all-hands meeting. Maybe if you hold off on the presentation…

Wait. Damn. You're supposed to be meditating, and here you are, thinking about work.

Does this sound familiar? If you've ever tried meditation, it probably will.

Meditation has changed my life, and so I recommend it to almost anyone who's willing to listen to me talk about it. And yet, when I bring it up, a lot of people say the same things.

I don't have time to meditate!

I can't just sit there and do nothing.

I can't turn my brain off and stop thinking.

The irony is, it's exactly the people who say things like this that could benefit the most from a regular meditation practice.

Every society throughout history has practiced some form of meditation. Meditation is natural to humans. Anyone is capable of meditating with enough practice.

Think of meditation as an exercise for your mind. If you haven't been to the gym in years, you don't expect to run a marathon, do you?

When you first start to meditate, you'll probably feel a bit awkward. You might wonder, *Isn't it boring? Am I just supposed to sit here? What does this actually accomplish? I have more important things to do!*

This is the first lesson that meditation teaches: patience and perseverance. In this chapter, I'll take you through several ways to meditate.

Sitting meditation

Start by finding a place where you feel comfortable. Most people choose a quiet place in their house, but you can meditate anywhere you want.

The ideal place is:

- **Peaceful:** Choose a place without too much noise. Turn off your phone or any other distractions.
- **Private**: You don't want people walking through and disturbing you while you meditate.
- **Safe:** You need to feel comfortable enough to let down your defenses.
- **Convenient:** Choose somewhere you can go every day. If you always meditate in the same place, your mind will begin to associate that place with conscious breath and deep concentration.

Wear loose clothing that you can sit and move around in comfortably. Yoga pants or sports clothes work pretty well.

How to focus:

You don't want to be distracted by checking the time, so decide how long you want to meditate for and then set the alarm on your phone. For your first time, five minutes is enough.

Ready? Close your eyes.

You can use any object to focus on when meditating – a mantra, a flame, an image – but it's easiest for beginners to start with their breath.

It's not because there's anything particularly magical about your breath. The reason meditators focus on their breath is because it's always with you, so you always have the means to meditate anywhere. You can't leave it behind when you go on vacation or forget it at the office.

As you breathe in, pay attention to the air that enters and leaves your lungs. Notice the rise and fall of your chest and torso. Devote all your attention to your breath.

As you sit in silence, random thoughts will cross your mind. You'll start to think about projects you're working on or what you're making for dinner. Let them go, neither clinging to them nor pushing them away.

Bring your attention back to your breath.

It's natural for the mind to wander a little bit. We get bored and start looking for things to think about other than our breath. When you notice this happening, don't worry. Remember that it's perfectly normal, and simply bring the mind back to your breathing.

As you come to the end of your meditation session, you can gradually come back to an awareness of your surroundings. Feel your body pressing into your chair or the floor, and feel the air moving through your lungs. What can you hear outside? What is happening around you?

Open your eyes.

Congratulations! You just finished your first meditation session.

Focusing exercises

With time and practice, it will be easier to keep your thoughts focused on your breath. If you're having trouble in the beginning, try one of these focusing exercises:

Counting

A mental chant helps you stay centered in your body. While breathing in, count one…one…one, then while breathing out count two…two…two…Once you reach ten, start again from one.

Another option is to silently say 'inhalation' as you breathe in and then 'exhalation' as you breathe out again. Keep going until you can focus on your breath without the need for words.

Body scan

Instead of focusing on your breath, in this meditation, you're going to move your attention over each part of your body. Start at the top with your head. Bring your attention to your eyes, ears, nose and mouth, then down to your neck and shoulders.

Consciously relax each muscle as you move your awareness down your body. Take note of any feelings – warmth, weight, itching – acknowledge the feelings, and then let them go.

Breathing awareness

Take a deep breath and then, as you breathe out, imagine the tension in your head and neck flowing down and out through your body. Your head becomes lighter on your shoulders.

As you release the next breath, imagine the tension flowing out of your shoulders and down your arms, then out through your fingertips. Work your way down through your torso and legs to the soles of your feet, gradually letting go of the tension.

A few other tips:

- Ease into it! If you're new to meditation, start out with only 5 to 30 minutes per day. You're more likely to maintain a regular meditation practice if you set a reasonable timeframe for yourself.

- Meditate every day. Don't skip days, or you'll struggle to establish a steady routine and reap the benefits. Try setting a regular time and place for your meditation, and prioritize it.
- Some people enjoy meditating with a like-minded community, a group of people who gather to meditate in silence together. If this interests you, check if there are any meditation groups in your area. Belonging to a group also increases your sense of accountability and may make you more likely to stick to your new practice.
- Many meditators enjoy the guidance of a meditation tape, especially when they are new to the practice. These tapes are plentiful, and you should be able to find one that's to your liking. To that end, I've compiled a list of mindfulness and meditation apps toward the end of this chapter.

Above all, don't pressure yourself! Meditation is not an activity like doing a job or playing a sport, and there's no way to be bad at it. Your mind will wander naturally, and you will lose focus. When it happens, don't beat yourself up about it. Just bring your attention back to your breath and the present moment.

Over time, this will become easier, but the goal of meditation is not to become better at meditating. It's simply to exist in the present moment and understand that this is all there is.

While you'll begin to experience benefits almost right away, the more you practice mindfulness through meditation, the greater the benefits will be. Once you get into it, you'll look forward to having that time to yourself and the deep relaxation that comes with meditation.

Once you're comfortable with sitting meditation, there are a few other positions you can try.

Walking meditation

Yes, you can meditate while walking! In fact, this is one of my personal favorite ways to meditate.

You want to walk somewhere relatively private. Indoors or in a quiet area of a park is fine. Choose somewhere with level terrain and no obstructions. For now, you want to focus on the movement of your body, rather than on navigating complicated terrain.

Walk slowly and with intention. Typically, we walk briskly without really thinking about it. In a walking meditation, you want to slow down and notice each component of the step.

You can break each step into four basic components:

- Lifting – lifting your foot off the ground.
- Moving – moving your foot forward.

- Placing – placing your foot back down on the ground.
- Shifting – shifting your weight from one foot to another.

Just like with breathing, you want to focus your conscious mind on the repetitive action. As you walk, think to yourself, *lifting… moving… placing… shifting…* Allow your eyes to remain open (you don't want to trip) but with soft focus.

As you walk, look at your surroundings. Notice that so-and-so who lives over there has a nice garden. Notice that there's a wasp's nest up in that tree. Notice that this house has been painted a new color. Notice the sounds and smells all around you: the noise of cars and buses, the conversations of other pedestrians, the songs of birds, the smell of flowers.

Taking the time to notice and observe your body as it moves through its environment centers you firmly in the present moment and gets you in touch with how you are doing and feeling that day.

Lying meditation

Lie on your back on a comfortable surface such as your bed or a yoga mat. Choose somewhere that gives you enough room to spread out comfortably. Just like with the sitting posture, imagine your spine is a piece of string being gently pulled into a straight line. Your legs should be about hip distance apart, and your hands relaxed, palms facing upwards, about a foot away from your hip.

You can leave your eyes open (with soft focus) or close them. Then use mindfulness techniques similar to those in the sitting and walking meditations.

- Concentrate on the feel of your chest as you breathe in and out
- Count your breaths as they come and go
- Scan down your body and take inventory of how it is feeling
- Feel the weight of your body as it presses into the ground or bed

Lying meditation is the best way to prepare your mind and body for sleep each evening. If you suffer from insomnia or have trouble letting go of the worries of the day, try lying meditation as a way to calm your mind.

Yoga

Yoga and meditation have been practiced together for thousands of years. There are many kinds of yoga such as Hatha, Kundalini, Yin, and Vinyasa. What they all have in common is that they promote mindfulness through stretching, balancing, and breathing.

Practicing mindfulness while you exercise is a great way to get in touch with your body, to notice how you move and sit. Used together, yoga and meditation will improve your posture, strength, flexibility, and breathing by making you mindful of your body.

Do you slump in your office chair? Are you holding your head at an awkward angle when you look at the screen? Awareness can help you adjust your position to work with your body instead of against it.

Yoga is a sort of moving meditation, a fantastic way to foster mindfulness. You learn to focus on the breath and bring all your attention inward. You let distractions go and learn to just slow down and settle into a steady rhythm.

The improved strength and flexibility that comes from yoga will help you cope with challenging positions and uncomfortable sensations during meditation. Mindfulness on your mat deepens the practice of yoga and allows you to truly relax.

I'm not going to delve into any yoga strategies here. Yoga is quite difficult to learn from a book, so I recommend taking a class from a qualified instructor or finding a video that you like and following along.

In saying that, while it is possible to perform yoga the same way you would any other exercise, I suggest bringing the same quiet, calm, mindful energy to yoga as you would to a sitting or walking meditation.

Ujjayi breath

Ujjayi breath is a holistic breathing technique in yoga which uses the entire respiratory system; diaphragm, rib cage, chest, and throat.

It is used in yoga to maintain rhythm during practice, and many people also say that it improves their concentration. Ujjayi exercises the lungs and increases the amount of oxygen in the blood. With practice, it can improve your lung capacity and give you greater control over your breathing.

How to do Ujjayi breath

- Start in a seated cross-legged position. Relax the body and close your eyes. Allow your mouth to drop open a little and relax your jaw and tongue.
- Bring to focus to the cycle of inhaling and exhaling deeply through your mouth. Notice the air and how it passes through your windpipe.
- When you inhale and exhale, contract the back of your throat as though you were whispering. As you breathe out, imagine yourself fogging up a window.
- You should produce a sound like ocean waves once you get the hang of the breath.
- Now close your mouth, breathing only through your nose.

- Focus on the sound of your breath, as it can relax your mind.
- Breathe in deeply, allowing your lungs to expand fully.
- Doing this breath for 15 minutes as a form of meditation is the ultimate way to bring focus inwards, promoting mindfulness.

List of Meditation Apps

If you're struggling to meditate regularly or having difficulty maintaining your focus, you could benefit a lot from using a meditation app. A guided session is a slightly easier way to start that helps you pull your focus back to the present, and daily reminders will help you stick to your routine.

- **The Mindfulness App:**
  http://themindfulnessapp.com/

This app starts you off with a five-day guided introduction to mindfulness, then offers an array of silent and guided meditation sessions that last between 3 and 30 minutes. There are statistics and daily reminders to help you practice consistently, and challenges to motivate more advanced practitioners. The premium version has several hundred additional guided meditations, plus courses on your body, sleep, and relationships.

- **Headspace:** https://www.headspace.com/

Headspace offers a free 10-part course in the basics of mindfulness and meditation, delivered in a series of short sessions between 3 and 10 minutes long. The sessions are jargon-free and easy to follow, and focus on the essentials of breathing and awareness. The premium version has hundreds of specialized meditations covering everything from sleeping better to reducing stress and dealing with anxiety.

- **Calm:** https://www.calm.com/

Apple's iPhone App Of The Year in 2017, Calm offers a range of relaxing sounds and visuals. There are guided Daily Calm meditations that help you refocus your attention, gentle outdoor sounds like waves breaking or a fire crackling, and music tracks designed to promote better concentration. You can even listen to a bedtime story read by the likes of Stephen Fry and Matthew McConaughey.

- **Insight Timer:** https://insighttimer.com/

Insight Timer is all about connecting you to a global community of meditators. There are thousands of groups where you can ask questions and offer advice, and a map so you can see people meditating nearby and invite friends to join you. They claim their library of free guided meditations is the largest on earth, with more than 15000 titles on everything from morning rituals to the yoga sutras.

- **10% Happier:**
  http://www.10percenthappier.com/

This is the most practical meditation app I've found; co-founder Dan Harris describes it as "no-bullshit". Harris is a news anchor who started meditating after he had a panic attack live on air. At first, he was skeptical, but after experiencing the benefits of meditation he became a convert. The guided sessions are all constructive and get straight to the point without any fluff, and are a great way to get the benefits of mindfulness "without the woo-woo".

Wrapping up

If the teachings of the Buddha provide the philosophical background of the spiritual practice, meditation, combined with mindfulness, is the practical application of that philosophy.

Creating a regular meditation practice can help you relax, but it can do much more for you than that. After all, meditation is a huge part of Buddhism, but it also has a place in most philosophical and spiritual traditions from around the world.

There's a reason for that.

Meditation offers you a way to bring Buddhist wisdom into your life on a daily basis.

That's what keeps this practice from being a dry philosophy and allows it to become an important part of daily life instead.

*

Epilogue: Answers for Life

What I want to show you in this book is simple: I want to show you how to live with maximum impact and minimum ego. Your ego doesn't need validation in order to achieve all your dreams. Nobody else needs to lose for you to make it to the top. Remember, there is enough room for everyone.

Because at the end of the day it's not about making it or not. It's about the present moment and the next step you take.

That's what I hope for readers to take from this book most of all.

You have power. You have far more potential, greatness, and happiness inside you than you might imagine.

The key to unlocking it isn't in positive thinking, detaching from life, or in spectacular plans for making $20 million dollars – although all the power to you if you do that!

The key to unlocking this power within is the next step you take.

The key isn't in your hands, it is *your hands*. You are the instrument of your own success.

By building a solid foundation inside yourself, you will guarantee that every step you take means something, even the ones that send you crashing to the ground and break your bones.

Make it mean something. Make it about more than yourself.

We grow strong when we line up our heart, mind, and body, and point them in a single direction; this is a triple-force multiplier. You want to be in the position of having all your energy lined up in one direction and knowing that you're not going back.

You will find others to work with on your path. You will have challenges you never expected. But once you embrace the fire that burns inside, you'll never be the same again.

Let me give you a clear comparison with this last short story:

Two young ladies win the same lottery at age 30 on opposite sides of the world.

The first young lady has always felt unsatisfied with life and wanted more. She believes she doesn't get the recognition she deserves. With the lottery win, she's now a multimillionaire. Her Instagram goes viral, catapulting her into worldwide fame. She meets what she thinks is the man of her dreams and is soon in a serious relationship. The whole world loves her.

Finally, she's gotten what she always wanted. Finally life is turning out the way she deserves.

The second young lady has always felt unsatisfied with life and wanted more, too. But she's also looked around her and noticed that everyone feels this way. It must be part of the human condition. She sympathizes with all the lonely souls who will never feel they belong or get what they deserve.

After winning the lottery, she starts a business expanding work opportunities for her community, becoming a leading philanthropist and developer of affordable housing. She's relatively unknown after the first blurb about her in the international media.

After five years, the first young lady has undergone numerous Botox surgeries and looks awful. She is broken up and on her tenth relationship with a handsome model. Her Instagram is a constant competition to stay ahead of her ratings. She feels completely alone and self-medicates with drugs to numb the pain and feel alive again. She was hoping money and fame would fill the void inside, but they just made it hurt even more. She got everything she thought she wanted, and it meant nothing in the end.

Meanwhile, after the same five years, the second young lady has met a local man who she's known since high school. They've always had a thing for each other and are now married and thinking about starting a family. Her community services are helping thousands, and she gets a warm feeling every time she sees somebody starting out with skills and confidence on the path of life.

The second young lady has always had an amazing heart, but without that lottery win none of this would have ever been possible! She sees it as a win for her whole community, not just her.

She got everything she wanted, and it all felt so meaningful in the end.

And that's what I'm saying here – if you work only for your own ego and pleasure, nothing you get will ever be enough.

Living with maximum impact and minimum ego is simple:

Live and work for a purpose beyond just yourself.

Live and work to your utmost ability and excellence because you can.

Help others because you have the ability to do so and this world already has more than enough pain, suffering, and misunderstanding without you adding to it. Practice lovingkindness because it's the right thing to do.

Have hope for the future because you have hope for right now.

And please don't forget the mud: the mud is where your roots grow.

If you're reading this on break at a job you'd rather not be at, in a marriage you'd rather not be in, in a hospital bed, or from the sofa where you're sitting wondering why life even matters, please don't give up on life just yet.

The mud is making you who you are. You are a human being with so much potential and value. Don't let anyone tell you otherwise. As author Og Mandino said – statistically and in every sense – you are the greatest miracle in the world.

Look, when you really think about it, there is such a high probability that you never would have existed. A lot of combinations clicked into place for you to be here today, reading this book and trying to make your life – your presence on earth – better. Isn't that mind-blowing?

If your life is in the dumps right now, this is my promise to you: it is going to get better, with your help.

If your life is amazing right now, this is my pledge: it is going to get even more fulfilling and fascinating.

What's next?

Connect with those around you and make your life matter. You will find satisfaction beyond your wildest dreams right here in our good, old world. As you let go of old ways of thinking and embrace these teachings, I'm confident you'll surprise yourself along the way.

Life will be even better than you could have imagined.

There is so much beauty in life's unknowns … enjoy its twists and turns, and know that each unexpected moment is a chance to grow and discover new strengths within yourself.

*

References

1. Science. "A wandering mind is an unhappy mind (2010)". https://pubmed.ncbi.nlm.nih.gov/21071660/

2. Crane, R. "Mindfulness-Based Cognitive Therapy (2017)". https://www.taylorfrancis.com/books/mono/10.4324/9781315627229/mindfulness-based-cognitive-therapy-rebecca-crane

3. Cognitive Therapy and Research. "The Impact of Intensive Mindfulness Training on Attentional Control, Cognitive Style, and Affect (2008)". https://www.researchgate.net/publication/226259406_The_Impact_of_Intensive_Mindfulness_Training_on_Attentional_Control_Cognitive_Style_and_Affect

4. Motivation and Emotion. "Mindfulness meditation and reduced emotional interference on a cognitive task (2007)". https://www.researchgate.net/publication/226504935_Mindfulness_meditation_and_reduced_emotional_interference_on_a_cognitive_task

5. Current Issues in Personality Psychology. "Mindfulness, relationship quality, and conflict resolution strategies used by partners in close relationships (2022)". https://www.ncbi.nlm.nih.gov/pmc/articles/PMC10653557/

*

SCAN ME

Made in the USA
Columbia, SC
16 August 2024